Proceedings of the 2009 BALEAP Conference

English for Specific Academic Purposes

Edited by
Siân Etherington

Published by
Garnet Publishing Ltd.
8 Southern Court
South Street
Reading RG1 4QS, UK

Published 2011.

ISBN: 978 1 85964 693-9

British Cataloguing-in-Publication Data
A catalogue record for this book is available from the British Library.

Production

Project consultant:	Rod Webb
Editorial team:	Peter Finn, Samantha Lacey, Jean McCutcheon
Design and layout:	Sarah Church, Mike Hinks, Bob House

Printed and bound
In Lebanon by
International Press.

Contents

Siân Etherington

Introduction

The biennial BALEAP conference brings together EAP professionals from the UK and further afield to discuss key issues in the teaching and learning of English for Academic Purposes. The 2009 conference held at Reading University was, as ever, a collegial and lively meeting where lecturers, teachers, materials writers and researchers gathered to exchange ideas, expand horizons and refresh enthusiasms. During the three days of the conference national and international delegates enjoyed 3 plenary talks and 60 presentations. Many thanks are due to the organizing committee for the smooth running and success of the conference.

The conference took as its theme 'English for Specific Academic Purposes'. It was felt that this theme allowed both a focus on a key issue of continuing interest to EAP professionals, and also permitted a degree of flexibility in application to a range of contexts. Indeed, Hyland in his opening plenary indicates some of the possible variations on this topic. He lists the specificity of language within different modes, the types of writing expected of students, cultural specificity in rhetorical practices, genre features and, the main focus of his lecture, specific language practices within academic disciplines.

It has perhaps been in this latter area that the question of specific teaching set against general or common core approaches has been most discussed in the EAP field. In their inaugural editorial for the first volume of the *Journal of English for Academic Purposes (JEAP)*, Hyland and Hamp-Lyons (2002:5–6) raise this as one of the major issues which the journal wishes to explore, and pose a set of questions prompting further investigation. Some of the questions focus on the research to be done to map the disciplinary specificity in genres; others address practical issues, such as the implementation of specific approaches within heterogeneous classes, or teachers' lack of discipline knowledge.

This interest has continued and grown: since 2002 EAP researchers have worked to expand understandings in these areas. Discipline-specific approaches to writing have been informed by a strong body of research using corpus linguistics. Researchers such as Hyland (e.g., 2000); Swales (e.g., 1990, 2004); and Nesi et al. (2004) have worked with academic corpora of various sizes to investigate the disciplinary use of linguistic features, organization of genres, and popularity and frequency of text types. Studies of learner corpora have also produced insights into the ways in which students themselves build their own sense of disciplinary expertise and sense of their place within a community of writers (e.g., Gilquin *et al* 2007). Research working more directly with students and academic staff has produced valuable taxonomies of genres used within disciplines, and also considered both student difficulties in writing particular texts for certain disciplines and how tutors can best support students in this sort of writing (e.g., Gimenez 2008 on texts in nursing and midwifery). Other teachers and researchers (e.g., Lee and Swales 2006) have investigated ways in which students themselves can become analysts of their own disciplines, suggesting valuable pedagogic developments in EAP writing curricula.

The papers in the present collection continue many of these themes, providing a valuable picture of current work on specificity and EAP and reflecting the variety and strength of presentations given at the conference. The collection is divided into four sections: the plenary talks are presented first, followed by three groups of papers which reflect common concerns from the conference talks.

In Section I the plenary lectures each bring the theme of specificity into focus in different ways. Ken Hyland's paper is clear about the importance of specificity, seeing it as 'the most central concept in language teaching and discourse analysis today'. He moves on to illustrate key differences between the use of particular linguistic features within hard and social sciences. The notion that the teaching of EAP is the teaching of a new and *discipline-specific* literacy is key to Hyland's paper. He argues that discipline communities are formed through the language practices they share, and it is these language communities which EAP teachers need to equip students to join.

Hilary Nesi considers the specific requirements of academic disciplines of their students' writing, relating this to the written assessments set within different departments. Her paper discusses the writing of one particular genre which often presents difficulties for students: the assessed reflective piece. Using data from the British Academic Written English (BAWE) corpus of student assignments, Nesi illustrates the writing strategies used by successful students in producing this genre, arguing that it is those students who learn 'the rules of the game' who score well in such writing.

Christine Feak's plenary paper charts the rise of interdisciplinarity within universities and considers the challenges this throws up for academics, students and EAP teachers. She describes the journey of one postgraduate student's 'self-initiation' into interdisciplinary work, showing how the student works to negotiate writing decisions with tutors from different disciplines and finally is able to use their often conflicting feedback to her own ends. The reminder that it is students themselves who are often the main providers of information to EAP tutors about discipline conventions is an important one.

The notion of 'specificity' also arises in various guises within the conference papers, and the three sections presented here reflect this. Papers in Section II use corpus analysis to research discipline variation within particular genres and the use of linguistic clusters within academic English. Section III centres on course design, where discipline knowledge and practice are researched to inform the development of teaching materials or approaches. The third group of papers (in Section IV) relates to EAP assessment, dealing with student preparation for specific tests, the management of particular types of assessment, and the use of different types of feedback.

In Section II, the first paper reports Philip Nathan's investigation into the use of modal verbs in business case reports. Accurate and appropriate use of modal verbs within reports of company actions and strategies has proven challenging for non-native writers and thus the paper centres on this area. The analysis of a small corpus of texts from both native and non-native speaker writers indicates differences in the ways in which each group employs patterns of verb use in certain stages of their writing. Differences in business specialisms also appear to influence the modal verb choice of writers.

David Qian and Yongyan Li's paper takes a similar approach and also centres on business writing. However, they discuss the use of clusters of language (or 'high frequency repeated word sequences') in an existing large-scale specialized corpus, the Hong Kong Financial Services Corpus. The paper identifies a number of high frequency clusters, each corresponding to a particular 'stage' in financial services writing. The authors argue that this set of clusters provides a valuable pedagogic tool for business writing teachers and learners. Together, these two papers provide useful models for teachers who may wish to carry out research on a classroom-based corpus.

The third paper in this group considers clusters of language use in academic writing in a somewhat different light. Mary Davis and John Morley's paper centres on the role of reusable phrases across postgraduate academic writing. The authors investigated postgraduate students' recognition and use of lexical chunks or formulaic constructions in academic writing, showing that students are able to recognize these chunks and see value in learning them. The study also indicated that students who use these sorts of phrases more frequently are more likely to gain good grades for academic writing. The paper ends with some discussion of the possible dangers related to the teaching of set phrases, but stresses their value for EAP curricula.

The first paper in Section III considers the introduction of a new text type into an existing writing syllabus. Benet Vincent and Müjde ener Nordling report on their work with faculty members to identify important aspects of the short answer text, their subsequent analysis of short answers against Horowitz's typology of examination texts (1986), and the development of teaching and assessment materials. The authors are candid about the challenges involved in this process, and their account represents a valuable framework for course development.

Sarah Horrod's paper covers similar territory, looking at the use of 'hybrid tasks' on marketing courses. These are assessment tasks which combine professional and academic demands, thus requiring particular writing approaches from students. Horrod worked with marketing academics to explore the particular challenges of this genre, in particular the differences which exist at 'sub-genre' levels. The discussion of the nature of writing within such 'newly vocationalized programmes' is a new and important avenue for many EAP tutors and researchers.

In the final paper in this section, Andy Gillett and Angela Hammond discuss course design of a pre-master's programme through a focus on assessment used in the target subject disciplines. Detailed analysis of the assessment types students will need to produce on their future courses informs the development of EAP teaching materials for the preparatory programme. The authors stress the importance of considering assessment at the early stages of course design. Their approach to balancing generic and subject-specific assessment needs provides a useful example of a particular syllabus response to the disciplinary requirements of EAP students.

Gillett and Hammond's paper provides a bridge between Sections III and IV, combining, as it does, issues involving both course design and assessment. Section IV focuses on assessment, including papers which investigate test preparation and the management of particular types of assessment. The first of these, Bruce Howell's case study, considers the tensions between very specific preparation for an EAP proficiency test (the Test of English for Educational Purposes) and more general preparation of students for UK study, arguing that a focus on the former does not necessarily preclude the other. Direct preparation for particular tests is often demanded by students during preparatory programmes, and Howell indicates that, although this may not directly benefit student proficiency scores, it is likely to bring other more long-lasting benefits, where such preparation is set within a broader EAP framework.

Test preparation is also the topic of Dorothy Adams-Metaxopoulou and Phil Morris's paper, which describes research into the support provided by language learning advisors to students preparing for the listening papers of the International English Language Testing System (IELTS) test. Advisors worked with students to reduce test anxiety in listening examinations, and results indicate an improvement in scores and reduction in anxiety for the students involved.

The paper by Ann Smith and John Hall describes a project to manage group assessment more fully, supporting students in the development of teamwork skills. Group work is an important assessment mechanism for many subject areas: in this research, the focus is on how Business and Social Sciences programmes help foundation students with this key but difficult skill. The authors illustrate a three-pronged approach, comprising the creation of a policy for dealing with disputes, the provision of training in group dynamics and collaboration, and the integration of authentic group projects within the content syllabus. Students are encouraged to reflect on the group dynamic and their own contributions throughout. Smith and Hall argue that many foundation students have little or no experience of group assessment, and thus this type of provision is of great value.

The rise of a particular approach to the testing of EAP skills and proficiency is considered in John Slaght's paper. Online testing is a fairly new phenomenon within the EAP context, and this paper provides a full and frank discussion of the advantages and disadvantages of this development.

Slaght raises important questions concerning, among other issues, the linguistic changes driven by increased online communication, the importance of live oral assessment in testing, and, most importantly, the consideration of the needs of test-takers. He concludes that computer-based testing has further to go before it becomes a normalized part of EAP assessment.

In the final paper in this collection, Jane Nolan and Elizabeth Poynter describe an action research project to improve teacher feedback, and evaluate student responses to feedback on written work. Student attitudes to written and audio feedback were collected through case study and questionnaires over an 18-month period. The paper shows how the introduction of new feedback systems required adjustment by both students and tutors throughout this time.

The 2011 BALEAP conference will take place in Portsmouth University under the title 'EAP within the HE Garden: Cross Pollination between Disciplines, Departments, Research and Teaching'. This promises an exciting continuation of some of the ideas and themes from the 2009 conference, as the focus moves from specificity to interdisciplinarity, alongside a consideration of other connections across and beyond the specific EAP context.

References

Gilquin, G., Granger, S., & Paquot, M. (2007). Learner corpora: the missing link in EAP pedagogy. *Journal of English for Academic Purposes*, *6/4*, 319–335.

Gimenez, J. (2008). Beyond the academic essay: Discipline-specific writing in nursing and midwifery. *Journal of English for Academic Purposes*, *7/3*, 151–164.

Horowitz, D. (1986). Essay examination prompts and the teaching of academic writing. *English for Specific Purposes*, *5/2*, 107–120.

Hyland, K. & Hamp-Lyons, L. (2002). EAP: Issues and Directions. *Journal of English for Academic Purposes, 1/1*, 1–12.

Hyland, K. (2000). *Disciplinary discourses: social interactions in academic writing*. London: Longman.

Lee, D. & Swales, J.M. (2006). A corpus-based EAP course for NNS doctoral students: Moving from available specialized corpora to self-compiled corpora. *English for Specific Purposes, 25/1*, 56–75.

Nesi, H., Sharpling. G., Ganobcsik-Williams, L. (2004). Student papers across the curriculum: Designing and developing a corpus of British student writing. *Computers and Composition*, *21/4*, 439–450.

Swales, J. M. (1990). *Genre analysis: English in academic and research settings*. Cambridge: Cambridge University Press.

Swales, J. M. (2004). *Research Genres: Explorations and Applications*. Cambridge: Cambridge University Press.

SECTION I

Plenary papers

Ken Hyland

Discipline and divergence: evidence of specificity in EAP

Specificity is perhaps the most central concept in language teaching and discourse analysis today and represents a key way in which we understand and practice EAP. My purpose in this paper is to offer some evidence for this statement, drawing on a range of research but particularly my own work in professional and student academic writing.

Dimensions of specificity

Specificity appears in numerous guises. Corpus studies undertaken by Biber (1988), for example, have confirmed Halliday's (1989) observations regarding the specificity of mode, finding greater nominalization, impersonalization and lexical density in written compared with spoken texts. There is also a high degree of specificity in the *kinds* of writing that students are asked to do, as surveys by Horowitz (1986) and others discovered. In fact, because different fields value different kinds of argument and set different writing tasks, even students in fairly cognate fields, such as nursing and midwifery, are given very different writing assignments (Gimenez, 2009). Similarly, research in contrastive rhetoric (e.g., Connor 2004) has pointed to cultural specificity in rhetorical preferences. While we can't simply predict the ways in which people are likely to write on the basis of assumed cultural traits, students' first language and prior learning come to influence ways of organising ideas and structuring arguments when writing in English at university.

Perhaps most research into specificity has attended to genre, where particular purposes and audiences lead writers to employ very different choices (e.g., Hyland, 2008). Table 1, for example, compares frequencies for different features in a corpus of 240 research articles and 56 textbooks.

Table 1 Selected features in research articles and textbooks

Per 1,000 words	Hedges	Self-mention	Citations	Transitions
Research articles	15.1	3.9	6.9	12.8
University textbooks	8.1	1.6	1.7	24.9

We can see considerable variation in these features across the two genres. The greater use of *hedging* underlines the need for caution and opening up arguments in the research papers compared with the authorized certainties of the textbook, while the removal of *citation* in textbooks shows how statements are presented as facts rather than claims grounded in the literature. The greater use of *self-mention* in articles points to the personal stake that writers invest in their arguments and their desire to gain credit for claims, and the higher frequency of *transitions*, which are conjunctions and other linking signals, in the textbooks is a result of the fact that writers need to make connections far more explicit for readers with less topic knowledge.

Overwhelmingly, however, it is *disciplinary* variation which underlies most specificity, and this is what I want to focus on here. Research on language variation across the disciplines is rapidly becoming one of the dominant paradigms in EAP (e.g., Hyland, 2004; Hyland & Bondi, 2006), and here specificity refers to the fact that we communicate as members of social groups, and that different groups use language to conduct their business, define their boundaries, and manage their interactions in particular ways. For EAP teachers this means focusing on communicating, and learning to communicate, as a disciplinary insider.

Specific vs general EAP

The importance of disciplinary specificity in academic literacy education is not new: Peter Strevens highlighted it as a defining feature of ESP in the early 1980s, for example, but there are still voices who deny the value of this kind of instruction, and instead argue for the teaching of general academic skills.

First, there is Ruth Spack's (1988) view that language teachers lack the training, expertise and confidence to teach subject-specific conventions, and that they should be left to those who know them best, the subject teachers themselves. Instead, EAP teachers should concentrate on general principles of study skills and rhetoric. Second, EAP is said to be too difficult for students with limited English proficiency, who need preparatory classes to give them a good understanding of 'general English' first. Third, there is a view that developing skills and familiarity with specific schemata amounts to a *training* exercise (Widdowson, 1983), a more restricted and mundane activity than *education*, which involves assisting learners to understand and cope with a range of needs. Finally, there is a widely held view that academic communication comprises a set of generic skills and language forms, which differ very little across the disciplines. Many EAP textbooks are based on this idea of a *common core* of grammar, and often courses are organized around themes such as 'academic writing' and 'oral presentations', which suggest that note-taking, essay-writing and speaking skills are similar in all courses.

In response, there are a number of objections to the EGAP position. For one thing, EAP teachers cannot rely on subject specialists to teach disciplinary literacy skills, as they generally have neither the expertise nor desire to do so. Second, the argument that weak students need to control core forms before coping with harder specific features of language is not supported by SLA research, which suggests that learners acquire features of the language as they need them, rather than in the order that teachers present them. Third, there are serious doubts over the existence of a 'common core' of language items. Focusing on a formal system ignores the fact that any form has many possible meanings, depending on its context, and by incorporating meaning into the common core we are led to the notion of specific varieties of academic discourse, and to the consequence that learning should take place within these varieties. Finally, it has been difficult to pin down exactly what *general* academic forms and skills actually are or how a set of common core features might help address students' urgent needs to operate effectively in particular courses, even if we could identify it.

In sum, there are advantages in trying to identify and teach whatever generic forms we can in contexts which do not allow us to specify students' needs clearly, such as in IELTS preparation courses or general pre-sessionals. Beyond that, however, we move away from the kind of research-based language instruction that we pride ourselves on, to something more vague and intuitive.

Disciplinary specificity

The idea of discipline has become important in EAP as we have become more sensitive to the ways in which genres are written and responded to by individuals acting as members of social groups. Ideas such as *communicative competence* in applied linguistics, *situated learning* in education, and *social constructionism* in the social sciences have contributed to a view which places community at the heart of writing and speech.

Essentially, we can see disciplines as language-using communities, and the term helps us join writers, texts and readers together. Communities provide the context within which we learn to communicate and to interpret each other's talk, gradually acquiring the specialized discourse competencies to participate as group members. It has to be admitted that the notion of discipline is not an altogether happy one. But while the concept is beset by challenges from post-modernists, who see intellectual fragmentation at every turn (e.g., Gergen & Thatchenkery, 1996), and from the emergence of practice-based and modular degrees, it is nevertheless a notion with remarkable persistence. I think, in fact, that the distinctive existence of disciplines can be informed by study of their rhetorical practices. This is because successful academic writing does not occur in an institutional vacuum. Instead, it largely depends on the individual writer's projection of a shared professional context as they seek to embed their writing in a particular social world which they reflect and conjure up through approved discourses.

So we can see disciplines as particular ways of doing things – particularly of using language to engage with others in certain recognized and familiar ways. Academic texts are about *persuasion*, and this involves making choices to gain support, express collegiality and resolve difficulties in ways which fit the community's assumptions, methods and knowledge. Academic discourse helps to give identity to a discipline. This means that we need to understand the distinctive ways they have of asking questions, addressing a literature, criticizing ideas and presenting arguments, so we can help students participate effectively in their learning.

Some example differences

I want to turn now to these disciplinary differences, and look at a series of studies I've done over the past decade or so into the features of a 1.5 million word corpus of research articles in 8 disciplines and 4 million words of student dissertations, together with interviews with 30 academics. I will briefly highlight a few of the disciplinary differences in these corpora.

Citation practices

One of the most striking differences in disciplinary uses of language is in citation practices. The inclusion of references to the work of other authors is obviously central to academic persuasion. This is because not only does it help establish a persuasive framework for the acceptance of arguments by showing how a text depends on previous work in a discipline, but it also displays the writer's credibility and status as an insider. It helps align him or her with a particular community or orientation, and confirms that this is someone who is aware of, and is knowledgeable about, the topics, approaches and issues which currently interest and inform the field. But because discourse communities see the world in different ways they also write about it in different ways, with Table 2 showing that two thirds of all the citations in the article corpus are in the Philosophy, Sociology, Marketing and Applied Linguistics papers – twice as many as in the science disciplines (Hyland, 1999). Basically, the differences reflect the extent

Table 2 Rank order of citations by discipline

Discipline	per 1,000 words	Discipline	per 1,000 words
Sociology	12.5	Biology	12.5
Philosophy	10.8	Electronic Engineering	8.4
Applied Linguistics	10.8	Mechanical Engineering	7.3
Marketing	10.1	Physics	7.4

Table 3 Most frequent reporting verbs

Discipline	Most frequent forms	Discipline	Most frequent forms
Philosophy	say, suggest, argue, claim	Biology	describe, find, report, show
Sociology	argue, suggest, describe, discuss	Elec. Eng.	show, propose, report, describe
Applied Ling.	suggest, argue, show, explain	Mech. Eng.	show, report, describe, discuss
Marketing	suggest, argue, demonstrate, propose	Physics	develop, report, study

writers can assume a shared context with readers. In Kuhn's (1962) 'normal science' model, natural scientists produce public knowledge through cumulative growth. Problems tend to emerge on the back of earlier problems, as results throw up further questions to be followed up with further research, so writers don't need to report research with extensive referencing. The people who read those papers are often working on the same problems, and are familiar with the earlier work. They have a good idea about the procedures used, whether they have been properly applied, and what results mean. In the humanities and social sciences, on the other hand, the literature is more dispersed and the readership more heterogeneous, so writers can't presuppose a shared context, but have to build one far more through citation.

This rather neat hard-soft discipline explanation is spoilt somewhat by the fact that Biology has the highest citation count per 1,000 words. Interestingly, this is largely due to a very high proportion of self-citation, with 13% of all citations to the current author compared with about 6% overall. There does, in fact, seem to be a considerable emphasis given to recognizing the ownership of ideas in Biology and showing how current research builds on the work of others, which makes it unusual among the sciences (Hyland, 2004).

Reporting verbs

There are also major differences in the ways writers report others' work, with results suggesting that writers in different fields draw on very different sets of reporting verbs to refer to their literature (Hyland, 1999). Among the higher frequency verbs, almost all instances of *say* and 80% of *think* occurred in Philosophy and 70% of *use* in Electronics. It turns out, in fact, that engineers *show*, philosophers *argue*, biologists *find* and linguists *suggest*. The most common forms across the disciplines are shown in Table 3.

These preferences seem to reflect broad disciplinary purposes. So, the soft fields largely used verbs which refer to writing activities, like *discuss, hypothesize, suggest, argue*. These involve the expression of arguments, and allow writers to explore issues discursively, while carrying a more evaluative element in reporting others' work:

(1) Lindesmith's (1965) classic work indicated the ...
Davidson defends this claim on the grounds that ...

Engineers and scientists, in contrast, preferred verbs which point to the research itself, like *observe, discover, show, analyze*, and *calculate*, which represent real-world actions:

(2) Edson et al (1993) showed processes were induced ...
... using special process and design, or by adding, or removing a mask.

This emphasis on real-world actions helps scientists represent knowledge as proceeding from impersonal lab activities rather than from the interpretations of researchers. Two scientist informants commented on this kind of use:

'Of course, I make decisions about the findings I have, but it is more convincing to tie them closely to the results.' (Physics interview)

'You have to relate what you say to your colleagues and we don't encourage people to go out and nail their colours to the mast as maybe they don't get it published.' (Biology interview)

The conventions of impersonality in science articles thus play an important role in reinforcing an objective ideology by portraying the legitimacy of hard science knowledge as built on socially invariant criteria. Again, it removes the author from the text to give priority to the unmediated voice of nature itself.

Hedges

Devices like *possible, might, likely* and so on, collectively known as hedges, also diverge across fields. These function to withhold complete commitment to a proposition, implying that a claim is based on plausible reasoning rather than certain knowledge. They indicate the degree of confidence the writer thinks it might be wise to give a claim, while opening a discursive space for readers to dispute interpretations (Hyland, 1996).

Because they represent the writer's direct involvement in a text, something that scientists generally try to avoid, they are twice as common in Humanities and Social Science papers than in hard sciences. So, we tend to find more statements like this:

(3) The existence of such networks did not go unnoticed by contemporaries (see Rocke, 1989), and it seems sensible to assume the men concerned were probably not unreflective about this patterned conduct either. (Soc.)
With hindsight, we believe it might have been better to have presented the questionnaire bilingually. (A.L.)

One reason for this is there is less control of variables, more diversity of research outcomes and fewer clear bases for accepting claims than in the sciences. Writers can't report research with the same confidence of shared assumptions, so papers rely far more on recognizing alternative voices. Arguments have to be expressed more cautiously by using more hedges.

In the hard sciences positivist epistemologies mean that the authority of the individual is subordinated to the authority of the text, and facts are meant to 'speak for themselves'. This means that writers often disguise their interpretative activities behind linguistic objectivity. They downplay their personal role to suggest that results would be the same whoever conducted the research. The less frequent use of hedges is one way of minimising the researcher's role, and so is the preference for modals over cognitive verbs. This is because modal verbs can more easily combine with inanimate subjects to downplay the person making the evaluation. So we are more likely to find examples like (4) in the sciences and those with cognitive verbs in the soft discipline fields (5):

(4) For V. trifidum, ANOVA showed a significant increase from L to L' and FI, which could be interpreted as reflecting the dynamics of fungal colonization. (Bio.)

The deviations at high frequencies may have been caused by the noise measurements (E.E.)

(5) I think this would be a mistake. (Soc.)

We suspect that the product used in this study may have contributed to the result. (Mkt.)

Scientists tend to be concerned with generalizations rather than individuals, so greater weight is put on the methods, procedures and equipment used rather than the argument. Modals, then, are one way of helping to reinforce a view of science as an impersonal, inductive enterprise while allowing scientists to see themselves as discovering truth rather than constructing it.

Self-mention

Finally, I want to discuss self-mention as a final important feature which varies across disciplines. This concerns how far writers want to intrude into their texts through use of 'I' or 'we', or to use impersonal forms. Presenting a discoursal self is central to the writing process, and we can't avoid projecting an impression of ourselves and how we stand in relation to our arguments, discipline, and readers. To some extent we have to see this as a personal preference determined by seniority, experience, confidence, personality, and so on, but the presence or absence of explicit author reference is a conscious choice by writers to adopt a particular community-situated authorial identity. However, my 240 research articles, once again, show broad disciplinary preferences with two-thirds of cases in the Social Sciences and Humanities papers (Hyland, 2001).

Table 4 Self-mention in research articles (per 1,000 words)

Philosophy	5.5	Physics	4.1
Sociology	4.3	Biology	3.4
Applied Linguistics	4.5	Mechanical Engineering	1.0
Marketing	5.5	Electrical Engineering	3.3
Average	**5.0**	**Average**	**2.9**

Now it's clear that writers in different disciplines represent themselves, their work and their readers in different ways, with those in the humanities and social sciences taking far more personal positions than those in the sciences and engineering. The reason for this is again that the strategic use of self-mention allows writers to claim authority by expressing their convictions, emphasizing their contribution to the field, and seeking recognition for their work (Hyland, 2001; Kuo, 1999). It sends a clear indication to the reader of the perspective from which statements should be interpreted, and distinguishes the writer's own work from that of others. Successful communication in the soft fields depends far more on the author's ability to invoke a real writer in the text, emphasizing their own contribution to the field while seeking agreement for it:

(6) 'I argue that their treatment is superficial because, despite appearances, it relies solely on a sociological, as opposed to an ethical, orientation to develop a response.' (Soc.)

'I bring to bear on the problem my own experience. This experience contains ideas derived from reading I have done which might be relevant to my puzzlement as well as my personal contacts with teaching contexts.' (A.L.)

So self-mention can help construct an intelligent, credible and engaging colleague by presenting a confident and authoritative authorial self.

In the hard sciences, as I noted earlier, researchers are generally seeking to downplay their personal role in the research in order to highlight the phenomena under study, the replicability of research activities, and the generality of the findings. Scientists, then, try to distance themselves from interpretations in ways that are familiar to most EAP teachers. Either using the passive voice (7), dummy 'it' subjects (8), or by attributing agency to inanimate things (9):

(7) This suggestion was confirmed by the observation that only plants carrying the pAG-I::GUS transgene showed a gain of GUS staining in leaves of clf-2 plants. (Bio. article)

(8) It was found that a larger stand-off height would give a smaller maximum shear strain when subjected to thermal fatigue... (M.E. article)

(9) The images demonstrate that the null point is once again well-resolved and that diffusion is symmetric. (Phy. article)

By subordinating their voice to that of nature, scientists rely on the persuasive force of lab procedures rather than the force of their writing. As this biologist told me:

'I feel a paper is stronger if we are allowed to see what was done without "we did this" and "we think that". Of course we know there are researchers there, making interpretations and so on, but this is just assumed. It's part of the background. I'm looking for something interesting in the study and it shouldn't really matter who did what in any case ... In theory anyone should be able to follow the same procedures and get the same results.' (Bio. interview)

In contrast, in the humanities and social sciences, the first person allows writers to strongly identify with a particular argument and to gain credit for an individual perspective:

'Using "I" emphasizes what you have done. What is yours in any

> piece of research. I notice it in papers and use it a lot myself.' (Soc. interview)
> 'The personal pronoun "I" is very important in philosophy. It not only tells people that it is your own unique point of view, but that you believe what you are saying. It shows your colleagues where you stand in relation to the issues and in relation to where they stand on them. It marks out the differences.' (Phil. interview)

By marking your views with the first person, you leave readers in no doubt of your stance, while claiming credit for what you are saying. It is a powerful way of demonstrating an *individual contribution* and establishing a claim for *priority*.

CONCLUSIONS

All the features I have presented here occur and behave in dissimilar ways in different disciplinary environments, and it is important that EAP course designers recognise this, with the most appropriate starting point for instruction being the student's specific target context. It reinforces the fact that students don't learn in a cultural vacuum, but are judged on their use of discourses that insiders are likely to find effective and persuasive. The ways that we use language are situated in domains of knowledge and ways of talking about knowledge, so that labels like reports, essays and oral presentations are not universals but just names that give our work a shorthand convenience.

The bottom line here is that EAP has nothing to do with topping up generic language skills. It is about developing new kinds of literacy; equipping students with the communicative skills to participate in particular academic cultures. The research I've reported here provides some evidence for this view. The fact that writers in different fields draw on different resources to develop their arguments, establish their credibility and persuade their readers means that EAP teachers need to take the disciplines of their students, and the ways these disciplines create texts, into account in their classroom practices.

References

Biber, D. (1988). *Variation across speech and writing*. Cambridge: Cambridge University Press.

Connor, U. (ed.) (2004). Contrastive rhetoric and EAP. Special issue. *Journal of English for Academic Purposes, 3/4*, 271–359.

Gergen, K. J. & Thatchenkery, T. J. (1996). Organisational science as social construction: postmodern potentials. *The Journal of Applied Behavioral Science, 32/4*, 356–377.

Gimenez, J. (2009). Beyond the academic essay: Discipline-specific writing in nursing and midwifery. *Journal of English for Academic Purposes, 7/3*, 151–164.

Halliday, M. A. K. (1989). *Spoken and written language*. Oxford: Oxford University Press.

Horowitz, D. M. (1986). What professors actually require: academic tasks for the ESL classroom. *TESOL Quarterly, 20/3*, 445–462.

Hyland, K. (1996). Writing without conviction? Hedging in scientific research articles. *Applied Linguistics, 17/4*, 433–454.

Hyland, K. (1999). Academic attribution: citation and the construction of disciplinary knowledge. *Applied Linguistics*, *20/3*, 341–367.
Hyland, K. (2001). Humble servants of the discipline? Self-mention in research articles. *English for Specific Purposes*, *20/3*, 207–226.
Hyland, K. (2004). *Disciplinary discourses*. Ann Arbor, MI: University of Michigan Press.
Hyland, K. (2008). *Academic discourse*. London: Continuum.
Hyland, K. & Bondi, M. (Eds.) (2006). *Academic discourse across disciplines*. Frankfurt: Peter Lang.
Kuhn, T. (1962). *The Structure of Scientific Revolutions*. Chicago: Chicago University Press.
Kuo, C-H. (1999). The use of personal pronouns: Role relationships in scientific journal articles. *English for Specific Purposes, 18/2*, 121–138.
Spack, R. (1988). Initiating ESL students into the academic discourse community: how far should we go? *TESOL Quarterly*, *22/1*, 29–52.
Widdowson, H. (1983). *Learning purpose and language use*. Oxford: Oxford University Press.

Hilary Nesi

Swimming with the sharks: helping students in infested waters

Introduction

This title is adapted from a comment made by a lecturer in History, interviewed in 2005 as part of the Economic and Social Research Council (ESRC)-funded project 'An Investigation of Genres of Assessed Writing in British Higher Education'. At the time the project team was particularly interested in exploring departmental expectations of student writers (Nesi & Gardner, 2006), but our History department representative refused to be drawn into any general pronouncements about how History assignments should be structured and signposted. Some colleagues liked significant points to be flagged up, he argued, while others disliked 'scaffolding', and did not feel the need for argument structure to be spelt out. This was just a fact of life which students had to learn to cope with – they had to 'learn to swim in shark-infested waters', using their own judgement about what style was likely to please what reader on any given occasion.

In some respects this was not a very helpful answer for the project team in their roles as EAP practitioners; we wanted to come away from the interview with some hard facts about the way History assignments should be written, information that we could relay to international students who were uncertain about so many aspects of British academic culture. The lecturer's comment stuck in my mind, however, because it carries an important message: ultimately students have to look out for themselves. Pre-sessional course tutors are sometimes guilty of keeping their students in the shallows until they are absolutely sure that they can swim, when instead they need to be helping them to develop the skills they need to survive alone in an unpredictable open sea.

Some time later, when we had completed another of our project tasks, the creation of the British Academy of Written English (BAWE) corpus of student assignments (e.g., Alsop & Nesi, 2009), we were able to gather examples of a written genre which presents particular risks for student writers, and for which the few guidelines available do not necessarily match the real expectations of assessors. This genre is the 'reflective piece', sometimes produced as an independent assignment, but more often included as a component of a larger task. This paper attempts to identify the strategies used by competent student writers in the production of this genre, strategies which will (perhaps) improve their chances of academic and employment success.

Reflective writing in the BAWE corpus

On the whole, assignments in the BAWE corpus draw on experimental data or academic readings, rather than the personal life of the writer. Their primary role is to evaluate entities, propositions or the behaviour of others rather than the behaviour of the self. The assignments thus conform to the 'essayist tradition', as described by Lillis (2001), in that they prioritize 'logic over emotion', 'competitiveness over collaboration' and 'academic truth over personal experience'.

Reflective pieces, on the other hand, differ markedly from all the other types of BAWE writing in that they focus on the personal development of the writer, often resulting from the writer's interaction with his or her peers. They may take the form of a diary, for example recording the writer's behaviour in practical sessions or during teamwork, or they may be an account of the writer's response to an overseas visit, coursework or patient care, a self-appraisal with regard to the writer's work performance, interviewing technique or career prospects, or a commentary on some other, non-reflective text that the writer has produced.

Although reflective pieces are so different from other types of BAWE writing, this does not mean that there is any quick way of identifying them in the corpus. The assignments which are solely reflective are fairly easy to find; they have been classed within the 'Narrative Recount' genre family, and tend to have titles which indicate their reflective purpose, for example 'Reflective piece for starting and running a business' (Narrative Recount: Engineering), and 'Individual reflective report on the process of teamwork and teamwork skills' (Narrative Recount: Health). Much reflective writing in the corpus is hidden within longer assignments which belong within other genre families, however, and the relevant section heading may or may not indicate the reflective content of the text. Such section headings include 'Feedback' (Essay: Computer Science), 'Personal career plan and reflective commentary' (Explanation: Hospitality and Leisure Tourism Management), and 'Learning process' (Critique: Business).

A trawl through all 2,761 assignments in the main BAWE corpus was therefore necessary in order to identify all the places where students had contributed writing in reflective rather than essayist mode. The resulting 'reflective subcorpus' consists of 59 texts ranging in length from 200 to 6,748 words, from 13 disciplines. The total size of the subcorpus is 86,795 words. The spread of texts across disciplines and levels of study (from first year undergraduate to master's level) is shown in Table 1.

Table 1 The reflective subcorpus

Discipline	Level one	Level two	Level three	Level four
Archaeology		✓		
Architecture				✓
Business			✓✓✓✓✓	
Chemistry			✓	
Computer Science	✓✓✓		✓✓	
Cybernetics	✓		✓	
Education		✓		
Engineering		✓✓✓✓✓✓	✓✓	✓
English				✓✓
Health	✓✓✓✓✓✓	✓✓✓✓	✓✓✓✓✓✓✓✓	
HLTM	✓	✓✓	✓✓	✓
Linguistics			✓✓✓✓	✓
Medicine (graduate intake only)				

Table 1 does not, of course, offer an exact record of the quantity of reflective texts required across the disciplines and levels. Such information cannot be derived from a corpus containing a limited number of assignments (roughly 200 texts at each level and in each disciplinary group, in the case of BAWE). It would in fact be very difficult to obtain this information by any means, given that lecturers are usually free to decide on their own assignment questions and vary them from year to year, and may also offer students a choice of tasks, some including reflection and others not.

Table 1 does, however, suggest that although reflective writing occurs in some 'pure' disciplines (Archaeology, Chemistry, English, and to some extent the computer sciences), it is most common in disciplines which prepare students for professions (Business, Education, Engineering, Health, Hospitality and Leisure Tourism Management (HLTM), (Applied) Linguistics and Medicine). As Squires (2005:130) points out, whereas students in the pure disciplines can pursue knowledge through experimentation under controlled conditions, events in the applied disciplines cannot be repeated, and so in order to improve their future practice, students have to reflect on their past performance.

The purposes of reflective writing

The idea of a 'reflective cycle' can be traced back at least as far as the work of Dewey (1859–1952), who believed that:

> ... inquiry should not be understood as consisting of a mind passively observing the world and drawing from this ideas that if true correspond to reality, but rather as a process which initiates with a check or

> obstacle to successful human action, proceeds to active manipulation of the environment to test hypotheses, and issues in a re-adaptation of organism to environment that allows once again for human action to proceed.
>
> (Field, 2005)

This experiential learning cycle of observing and recording problems, critically analyzing them, forming and testing hypotheses and implementing change has since been extensively discussed by Kolb (1984), Schön (1987, 1991) and Moon (1999), amongst others. Reflection has for many years been central to the creative development of artists (e.g., Getzels & Csikszentmihalyi 1976) and health professionals (e.g., Johns 2004). Also, despite the fact that the original concept of experiential learning owes much to scientific research methods, reflection has come to be a crucial tool in qualitative research, where the personal circumstances and attitudes of the researcher need to be critically self-examined, because they will inevitably have some bearing on the research outcome (e.g., Mruck & Breuer, 2003).

In the UK, reflection has recently become more prominent across a wider range of disciplines as part of Personal Development Planning (PDP), an initiative promoted by the Quality Assurance Agency (QAA) and other higher education committees, and sparked by concerns raised in the 1997 Dearing Report (Varnava, 2008). PDP equates reflection with the development of transferable skills, the idea being that students who reflect and plan will better meet the requirements of employers, and that the evidence of reflection and planning that students provide will enable employers to select them from an increasingly large pool of applicants with similar qualifications.

Herein lies a conflict, because although they might have their roots in the same educational philosophy, reflection as a tool towards self-discovery is not quite the same thing as reflection as a means of convincing others of one's self-awareness. This is evident in the different demands educationalists and potential employers make of reflective writers. According to Schön (1987:1) reflection is necessary to solve 'messy' and 'confusing' problems, but graduates applying for their first job will probably be wary of dwelling on the 'swampy lowlands' of everyday professional practice. The graduate job market emphasizes instead the positive outcomes of reflection; the following excerpt from an application form is typical in the way it asks students to:

- Tell us about an experience and feedback, which you feel significantly impacted on your development ...
- Give us an example of when you have worked successfully as part of a team or in a partnership. In your example explain clearly the relationships and interactions that took place ...
- Describe for us a time of complex change when you were expected to take on new tasks and responsibilities.

(*British Gas Graduate Programme*, 2009)

As we shall see, much of the writing in the reflective subcorpus seems to serve as a rehearsal for the job interview or job application. Under the guise of reflection, students are learning to present themselves to good advantage as team players and innovators, revealing qualities that are not assessed in the examination hall.

Strategies for reflective writing

Although all the assignments in the BAWE corpus were submitted for assessment, it is difficult to tell the extent to which short reflective sections in longer assignments affected the students' final marks. One suspects that many markers simply checked that a reflective section had been included, without evaluating its content. Nevertheless, it is easy to see why students should feel uncomfortable about the assessment process. It is inherently face-threatening, requiring writers to reveal rather private personal information to a socially distant and more powerful reader. Moreover, the final product, full of anecdotal evidence and personal references, may appear unscholarly – the kind of writing students have spent most of their life learning to avoid. Platzer et al (2000), Johns (2004), Evans (2007) and Ecclestone & Hayes (2009) all report student resistance to assessed reflection, summed up in these comments from a third year theatre student (Evans, 2007:71):

> 'The point of journals is to be free to express my thoughts and feelings without constraint. How can I be totally free to express myself when I have to make this piece of work comply to set regulations and guidelines? Why should I have my true feelings marked and graded?'

In order to 'swim with the sharks', students somehow have to indicate participation in the reflective cycle, with its 'messy, confusing problems' (Schön 1987:1), yet also present themselves in a good light, as students and as members of their profession. How do they achieve this? Analysis of the reflective subcorpus reveals that they tend to make strategic choices concerning both the linguistic features and the structure of their accounts. Good outcomes are attributed to the writer, the responsibility for problems is shifted elsewhere, the reader's sympathies for the writer are aroused, and stories end on an upbeat note, signalling readiness for the world of work.

A common tactic is to ascribe to the first person positive feelings that the reader might approve of, as in Examples 1 and 2:

Example 1

> This assignment has left me with <u>a genuine interest</u> in the area of international strategies and strategic thinking. (0155b)

Example 2

> Posting on fora is not something I tend to do, but it was strangely <u>enjoyable</u>. (6101c)

Negative feelings are ascribed to the first person when they suggest vulnerability rather than aggression or indifference. Outside agencies are often blamed for causing the writer's distress, either implicitly, as in Examples 3 and 4, or explicitly, as in Examples 5, 6, 7 and 8:

Example 3

> <u>I was a bit nervous</u> because we were the first group to go, and I felt slightly disadvantaged. (0424c)

Example 4

Term 2 was a shock to me. It was an intellectually confusing phase and it shook my beliefs and raised plenty of doubts. (0206e)

Example 5

One area I found difficult was that sometimes too much was expected of me in terms of my ability. (3101d)

Example 6

I was upset that the person who was supposed to work on that aspect didn't look into it … (0354a)

Example 7

I found it very frustrating that she didn't contribute to group communications. (3092d)

Example 8

Joe was in charge of the finances; Ben was all over the design. Apart from this, the other two didn't really do much. I was quite disappointed that they wouldn't get more involved. (0347g)

Examples 6, 7 and 8 in particular, indicate the dilemma the writers face when reflecting for assessment purposes. They blame other team members to justify their own behaviour and protect their own self-esteem, yet in so doing they fail to provide any evidence that they have learnt from their experiences. Failure is not attributed to causes they can control (Weiner, 1986), but this presumably means that the writers would be just as upset, frustrated and disappointed next time they found themselves in similar circumstances. Some writers discover subtle ways of acknowledging problems without dwelling on their own personal failings. In Example 9 the writer's teamwork and listening skills deficits are implied, but are presented as indicative of independence; a positive attribute.

Example 9

I feel the interview also gave us an opportunity to build on our team building skills and organisational skills. I, however, feel that I am a very independent person and I work better on my own. Yet within this profession it's not possible to work on my own and so it has helped me to try and improve my skills and confidence of working within a group and learning to listen to other people's opinions. (3059a)

Another way of downplaying personal failings is to disguise the agency of actions through passivization, as in Example 10, where poor time management skills are only obliquely acknowledged:

Example 10

It is not envisaged that any specification changes would be necessary, but it is possible (as the author has little previous experience in these areas) that the time required has been underestimated and therefore that these phases may take longer than anticipated. (0263f)

The impersonal 'It … have been' occurs 14 times in the subcorpus, and serves as another means of avoiding full acknowledgement of responsibility, as in Examples 11–13:

Example 11

It could be argued that by using the word 'dispute' we immediately made the interviewee feel anxious and it may have been better for us to be more general about the content of questions we were going to ask. (3030b)

Example 12

Ideally it would have been beneficial to record the interview on a camcorder. (3069b)

Example 13

Also at the beginning of the interview it would have been better to state how long it was likely to last. (3030b)

In these examples, the construction is a substitute for 'I should have' or 'we should have', which seem to be riskier claims. Of the two, 'we should have' is much more common because it allows the writer to share responsibility with others, as in Examples 14 and 15:

Example 14

This was possibly an issue we should have addressed early in order to maintain some professionalism and structure to the group. (0354a)

Example 15

In hindsight we should have mentioned the noise levels during our interview. (3030b)

'I should have' acknowledges sole responsibility for mistakes, and is usually hedged to minimise self-criticism, as in Example 16.

Example 16

Personally, I have to admit that, *because of the fact that I lacked the practice that input and output offers to a learner*, I should have invested more time and effort to the learning process. (6024a)

Alongside these various strategies to gain sympathy or approval, and to minimise the impression of culpability for their actions, many of the writers structure their reflective accounts to create a satisfactory narrative of triumph over adversity. Negative emotions and practical difficulties are recorded early on in the process, followed by expressions of self-confidence and capability. The future is usually viewed optimistically, just as it might be in a job interview, as in Examples 17–19 ('I will be able to' is one of the commonest lexical clusters in the subcorpus):

Example 17

I have spent 10 sessions in each section. They have taught me lessons that I will be able to use in the future, in my career in the hospitality industry. (3101b)

Example 18

I hope that in future I will be able to creatively engage in professional work. (3113a)

Example 19

I am acutely aware of the increased expectations of third year students and the impending expectations of qualifying and hope that by focusing on a personal characteristic I feel needs attention I will be able to develop both personally and professionally. (3092g)

Conclusion

It is evident from the above discussion that the competent writers featured in the BAWE corpus used a wide range of linguistic resources in order to present themselves in an appropriate light, as reflective students and as reflective job applicants. Evans (2007:75) is suspicious of reflective pieces that seem too 'polished', because it is possible that 'tidying up uncertain situations and unassociated ideas may be indicative of a failure to deal with the complexity of the world, and a desire to assert the self, rather than reveal/discover it'. Indeed, we cannot be sure whether the BAWE student writers had always reflected deeply on their experiences, or whether their claims were sometimes merely strategic. Perhaps our role as EAP practitioners does not extend to ensuring sincerity, however. Perhaps, if we introduce our students to the techniques used by successful writers to talk about their personal development, we will have done enough, by providing them with the resources they need to compete with their peers, and to 'swim with the sharks'.

Acknowledgement

The British Academic Written English (BAWE) corpus was developed at the Universities of Warwick, Reading and Oxford Brookes under the directorship of Hilary Nesi and Sheena Gardner (formerly of the Centre for Applied Linguistics [previously called CELTE], Warwick), Paul Thompson (Department of Applied Linguistics, Reading) and Paul Wickens (Westminster Institute of Education, Oxford Brookes), with funding from the ESRC (RES-000-23-0800).

References

Alsop, S. and Nesi, H. (2009). Issues in the development of the British Academic Written English (BAWE) corpus. *Corpora, 4/1*, 71–84.

Cotton, A. H. (2001). Private thoughts in public spheres: issues in reflection and reflective practices in nursing. *Journal of Advanced Nursing, 36/4*, 512–519.

Ecclestone, K. & Hayes, D. (2009). *The dangerous rise of therapeutic education*. London: Routledge.

Evans, M. (2007). Another kind of writing: reflective practice and creative journals in the performing arts. *Journal of Writing in Creative Practice, 1/1*, 69–76.

Field, R. (2005). John Dewey (1859-1952). In J. Fieser & B. Dowder (Eds.), *Internet Encyclopedia of Philosophy*. [www.iep.utm.edu/dewey/].

Getzels, J. W., & Csikszentmihalyi, M. (1976). *The creative vision: Longitudinal study of problem finding in art*. New York & London: John Wiley and Sons.

Gibbs, G. (1988). *Learning by doing: A guide to teaching and learning methods*. Oxford: Further Education Unit, Oxford Polytechnic.

Johns, C. (2004). *Becoming a reflective practitioner* (2nd edition). Oxford: Blackwell Publishing.

Kolb, D. A. (1984). *Experiential learning: experience as the source of learning and development*. Englewood Cliffs, NJ: Prentice Hall.

Lillis, T. (2001). *Student Writing: access, regulation, desire*. London: Routledge.

Moon, J. (1999). *Reflection in learning and professional development: theory and practice*. London: Kogan Page.

Mruck, K. & Breuer, F. (2003). Subjectivity and reflexivity in qualitative research. *Forum: Qualitative Social Research, 4/2*, Art.17, [www.qualitative-research.net/index.php/fqs/article/view/696].

National Association of Primary Care Educators (2005). *Introduction to GP Appraisals*. PDP Toolkit [www.pdptoolkit.co.uk].

Nesi, H. and Gardner, S. (2006). Variation in disciplinary culture: university tutors' views on assessed writing tasks. In R. Kiely, G. Clibbon, P. Rea-Dickins, & H. Woodfield (Eds.) *Language, Culture and Identity in Applied Linguistics* (British Studies in Applied Linguistics, 21). (pp. 99–117). London: Equinox Publishing.

Platzer, H., Blake, D. & Ashford, D. (2000). Barriers to learning from reflection: a study of the use of groupwork with post-registration nurses. *Journal of Advanced Nursing, 31/5*, 1001–1008.

Schön, D. (1987). *Educating the reflective practitioner: toward a new design for teaching & learning in the professions*. San Francisco: Jossey-Bass.

Schön, D. (Ed.) (1991). *The reflective turn*. New York: Teachers College Press.

Squires, G. (2005). Art, science and the professions. *Studies in Higher Education, 30/2*, 127–136.

Varnava, T. (2008). PDP update: policy and practice. The Higher Education Academy. [www.ukcle.ac.uk/resources/pdp/varnava.html].

Weiner, B. (1986). *An attributional theory of motivation and emotion*. New York: Springer-Verlag.

CHRISTINE B. FEAK

CULTURE SHOCK? GENRE SHOCK?

INTRODUCTION

EAP teaching in higher education settings generally has one central focus, namely helping students acquire the academic literacy skills needed to succeed in their chosen field of study. To this end, many EAP courses are directed at providing students with opportunities to become familiar with, and ideally acquire, discipline-specific rhetoric and language. How this is best done has been the focus of much debate over the years, leading to a number of questions. Is there a common core of features around which to create EAP courses? Do skills addressed in an EAP course transfer to other settings? Is EAP coursework most effective with students from the same or different disciplines? How much knowledge of various disciplinary traditions do EAP instructors need? To what extent can or should EAP courses emphasize socializing students into their chosen field? Does EAP teaching simply accommodate the status quo and in that sense constrain students? Complicating efforts to answer these questions are changes in the fabric of the disciplinary communities to which our students, particularly postgraduates, strive to belong. The lines between disciplines are becoming increasingly blurred and becoming so as a result of a number of factors, including university administrations, who want their institutions to be at the forefront of change. A recent announcement by my own institution likely echoes the sentiments of many other institutions of higher learning:

> '... one must also recognize that the disciplines themselves are fluid, and that the cross-pollination of interdisciplinary work has been one of the main historical determinants of their evolution and current profile. Failure to understand this inherent fluidity can lead to disciplinary complacency, or even arrogance. Disciplinary

> conservatism can breed contempt for colleagues who are committed to interdisciplinary work, viewing them as "marginal" rather than "cutting edge". (Subcommittee on Interdisciplinarity, 1999)

Establishing a single disciplinary identity was once something to strive for. Today however, this notion, as well as the traditional divisions among departments, is being challenged (Reis, 2000).

Another look at my own institution provides further evidence that the emphasis on interdisciplinary work is indeed quite strong, and growing. For instance, a search for the term *interdisciplinary* on the University of Michigan website will yield more than 71,000 hits for the term, an increase of 20,000 in the past 12 months. Further, no fewer than 115 interdisciplinary programmes have been created in recent years, ranging from Financial Engineering to Environmental Sustainability to Microbial Ecology. Consistent with this growth, recently established is a five-year, $30 million university initiative to hire 100 new junior faculty with interdisciplinary interests.

An emphasis on interdisciplinary work is also prevalent among funding agencies. Increasingly, research funding is awarded to interdisciplinary work, which is expected to work on 'big picture' issues such as environmental change (Committee on Science 2004). Funding for interdisciplinary work has in turn led to an exponential increase in publications of that nature. One 2007 study of the Web of Science database demonstrates a growing tendency toward interdisciplinary work over the past 25 years (Braun & Schubert, 2007), which the US National Academy of Sciences largely attributes to the following:

- the inherent complexity of society
- the desire to explore problems and questions that cannot be confined to a single discipline
- the need to resolve societal problems
- the power of new technologies (Committee on Science 2004)

The emphasis on interdisciplinary work varies from country to country and across disciplines (Braun and Schubert ibid.) and is by no means a US phenomenon. Apart from the US, at the forefront of interdisciplinary research are Germany, England, Canada, France, Italy and the Netherlands (ibid.). In terms of areas of such research, medicine, education and public health are the most prolific.

With the growing emphasis of interdisciplinary work, the challenges that postgraduate students face as they develop the academic literacy skills needed to succeed in a postgraduate degree programme are becoming increasingly complex. Interdisciplinary work 'thrusts graduate students into not one but a multitude of discourse communities' (O'Regan and Johnson, 2001), leaving them to contend not with a single cultural entity, but rather with what Becher and Trowler (2001) describe as 'academic tribes and territories', each with its own traditions and idiosyncratic practices.

To say that these many 'tribes' may be a potential source of confusion is perhaps an understatement. On the surface, the different discourse communities may appear homogeneous to unsuspecting students who move in and out of them, not recognizing the thinking, reading and writing practices specific to each discipline. New postgraduate students in particular may be left to demystify the different cultures on their own, since even their own advisors may not possess the discoursal expertise needed to offer some assistance (Swales, 1990; Swales & Feak, 2000). Further, as Zhu (2004) points out, although one might assume that content instructors will help students become aware of the 'unique thought processes' and disciplinary traditions that are embodied in academic writing, this is not necessarily the case. Content instructors may indeed provide students with frequent opportunities for writing, but they may not discuss the nature of writing processes with them, instead focusing on matters of content. Subject specialists often view academic writing conventions as self-evident (Lea & Street, 1999) and thus are not necessarily able to help their students acquire (inter) disciplinary skills. Indeed, Zhu found that faculty members viewed their role in teaching academic writing as secondary to teaching content and technical skills. Since academic literacy instruction does not necessarily occur in content courses, Hyland (2002) argues that ESP courses must teach 'the literacy skills which are appropriate to the purposes and understandings of particular communities'. This specificity must be central in order to help students 'to see the complex ways in which discourse is situated in unequal social relationships and how its meanings are represented in social ideologies' (Hyland, 2002).

The extent to which we can and need to delve into matters of specificity, however, largely depends on the students in our EAP writing (and other) classrooms. The reality is that, for various reasons, EAP teaching efforts are primarily directed toward less proficient students who often are in their first or second semester of their postgraduate programmes and who, for some reason, are often required to take our EAP courses. Baseball caps pointed backward, they sometimes even dare us to offer them anything of value (they soon realize that we will, of course). If they are not engaged in any significant writing project, students in their first or second semester may not yet quite be ready to be dealing with issues of discourse communities, disciplinary identity and alternative framings of discourse. Some postgraduate students have little discourse terrain to negotiate if their goal is to take coursework (particularly courses which require little or no writing), earn their Master's degree and then enter the 'real world', leaving academia behind. While we want to offer EAP support for these students, we often do not see those who may be most in need of support. Postgraduates with high Test of English as a Foreign Language (TOEFL) scores are generally viewed as capable of managing without any EAP support. Such students are not directed into EAP coursework, but are often left to struggle with the process of self-initiation into various discourse communities. However, lacking explicit guidance, these students – many of whom are working in interdisciplinary programmes – are no less disadvantaged than those in our courses 'as they are confronted with multiple ... discourses, content, and assumptions about the nature of academic writing and about disciplinary participation' (Hyland, 2000).

To discuss this matter further, I will now turn my attention to a postgraduate student, Mimi, who was attempting on her own to navigate the process of self-initiation into her interdisciplinary research community.

ONE STUDENT'S JOURNEY OF SELF-INITIATION INTO INTERDISCIPLINARY WORK

In many ways Mimi (a pseudonym, of course) is typical of many strong doctoral students, having earned a Master's degree from one of the top universities in Korea. She was accepted into the PhD programme at the University of Michigan, which is a joint degree programme integrating social work with one of five social science disciplines: Anthropology, Economics, Political Science, Psychology and Sociology. Mimi elected Sociology as her second discipline. Like many students, her experience of writing in English was limited, consisting primarily of statements of purpose for applications to PhD programmes. Despite her limited writing experience, because of her high TOEFL score (well over 100 on the IBT TOEFL or equivalent to over a 7 on the IELTS) Mimi was exempt from the university's in-house academic English evaluation and EAP coursework.

Mimi was also typical in that she thought she should not bother her advisor with writing in progress. As she put it, 'My advisor should be the end of the road. How I get there is my struggle'. Yet, by the middle of her second year of study she began to have serious doubts about her ability to succeed, as a result of frustrations with her preliminary exam proposal – a student's last major exam prior to achieving candidacy and the next to last step before completing the doctorate. The proposal consists of a comprehensive literature review on an issue of critical importance chosen by the student, a set of research questions and an outline for conducting the research.

Highly motivated to achieve candidacy, Mimi did not delay working on her preliminary exam, as students are wont to do. In fact, she had a topic that her advisor had in principle approved, namely factors that influence the decision of Korean women to return to work after they have a child. She also had developed a rather creative strategy to finish the proposal by the end of her second year. This involved enrolling in courses that required a final paper and negotiating the final paper with instructors of those courses so that she could in effect submit what would be her proposal. In this latter regard, she was certainly not typical.

In her second semester Mimi enrolled in an anthropology seminar that required drafts of the final paper to be turned in at different points during the term. These drafts were critiqued by a small group of students as well as the professor. Her first draft focused on the Korean employment context, but given the paucity of research on Korea, it drew from the US-based literature for support. The feedback on her midterm draft was very negative. Mimi reported, 'They really didn't like it and they said why do you want to focus on Korea when there is no research? The student group and the professor urged me to focus on the US. I could see the problem and so I thought so too. I thought how can I do this and maybe I am too narrow. But still I was interested in Korea and I didn't want to give it up'.

She revised her work so that the Korean context was de-emphasized. The second draft received negative criticism again, mainly because there was still too much emphasis on Korea. Frustrated, she revised again. Below is an excerpt from her final paper.

> *Theoretical and Empirical Understanding of Parental-Leave Policy and Women's Employment after Child Birth in Korea*

> ... The purpose of this proposal is to analyze and integrate theoretical and empirical studies of the effects of family leave policies on maternal employment after childbirth. The focus of this prelim exam is on governmental family leave policies.
>
> Sociologists, demographers, and economists have analyzed the relationship between maternal employment and child bearing or child rearing. It has been widely documented that having a baby decreases a woman's labor attachment (Desai, 1991; Leibowitz, 1995; Leibowitz, 1992; Nakamura, 1994; Nakamura, 1999). This is an interesting situation for Korea as well.
>
> To participate in the labor force women, who typically care for children, should limit their fertility or make alternative arrangements for the care of their children (Leibowitz, 1992). Many industrialized countries face the lower fertility rates which are below the replacement level with a rising proportion of women participating in the labor market. Concern with endemic lower fertility and slow increase in female employment rates in Korea has stimulated interest among researchers and policy makers in the relationship of motherhood to maternal employment and the impact of child care policy on this relationship.

Although Mimi did not entirely abandon her focus on Korea, what had initially been her primary interest had become almost inconsequential. Despite the effort to downplay the Korean focus, the criticism persisted and Mimi received a 'B', which for a US postgraduate student often indicates less than satisfactory work. In her feedback, the anthropology professor wrote that Mimi should:

- drop the Korean focus since there is no connection to the literature review
- focus on the United States or some western country where there is abundant literature
- find her voice
- work on the connection of ideas

In a final comment, the professor indicated that Mimi 'needed to improve her grammar' so that her writing would be clear – a typical catchall comment that one might question here. Clearly, the professor did not see how she might in fact play a role in helping Mimi gain a better understanding of how discipline-specific writing is shaped by unique thought processes and conventions. The comments offer a concrete content suggestion – drop Korea – but no discussion as to why the lack of literature should prompt a shift in Mimi's focus. Not surprisingly, no explanation was given as to how Mimi was to find her voice, while abandoning a topic about which she was passionate. Nor was any useful guidance offered as to what regarding her grammar needed improvement.

Mimi viewed her performance in Anthropology as a failure. She concluded that the Anthropology professor (and the students no less) correctly identified the big mistake of trying to keep the Korean connection. She also was convinced that, because her grammar was bad, her writing must be bad. Mimi revised her work over the semester break and at the beginning of the second semester she enrolled in a Sociology seminar. Again she persuaded the professor to allow her to submit her preliminary exam paper rather than the assigned research paper. Convinced her English was insufficient to meet the demands of her PhD programme, Mimi also enrolled in my 'Dissertation Writing and Writing for Publication' course, hoping to find the kind of 'quick fix' that is often associated with EAP coursework. Early in the semester we met to discuss her newly revised proposal that painstakingly incorporated the suggestions from the Anthropology class.

In our first appointment to discuss the proposal, Mimi and I talked about her research interests and her future plans. At this time she revealed that she wanted to do research on Korean women and employment. This was surprising since the paper she had just sent to me had nothing to do with Korea. Mimi recounted her experience in the Anthropology class, explained that she had to choose either the US or the Korean context, and indicated that, since there was little published work on Korea, she felt compelled to abandon her interest in Korea and choose the US. Mimi also described how she was continuing with her strategy for finishing the preliminary examination paper, adding that getting advice from the Anthropology professor or the Sociology professor would be equivalent to getting advice from her own advisor. However, the advantage was that she could submit her work to her advisor without burdening her along the way.

Here I provide an excerpt from the first text we discussed.

> *Leave Policy and Women's Employment after Childbirth*
>
> The purpose of this preliminary exam is on the effects of childcare leave policies on maternal employment following childbirth. The focus of this exam is on governmental child-care leave policies – i.e., I do not attempt to understand the effects of employer's provisions in regard to child-care. I will analyze and integrate theoretical and empirical research on how childbirth affects mother's employment and whether child-care leave policies affect the employment behaviors.
>
> Human capital theory has emerged to explain the negative relationship of fertility to female employment and earnings. To understand how childcare influences female labor supply, two streams provide insight. One emphasizes reward and value. For instance, Blau and Ferber (1992) posit that family responsibilities such as childcare increase the value women place on time in the home, making staying at home more preferable for mothers. On the other hand, the other focuses on the cost of having child care and views it as a family tax on women's employment and wages (Cooke, 2001; 9).

No doubt Mimi had successfully removed any vestiges of her interest in Korea as well as any voice that might have been present in the previous version of her paper, thus, in my mind, revealing a flaw in her writing strategy. Interestingly, Mimi was not particularly interested in my suggestion that, even while considering the earlier comments on her work, she could perhaps reconsider her newfound focus, and that we work on reshaping the paper to reflect her actual research interest. She acknowledged that her current version made her more dependent on the ideas of others and limited her options, but wanted to follow the Anthropology professor's feedback because it felt like a safe choice that might prevent yet another 'failure'. She stated that she would 'prefer to work on newly revised text' in terms of grammar and the connection of ideas.

Given that her paper was complete, I suggested that she at least discuss the proposed work with the professor of her Sociology course early in the semester rather than wait to receive feedback; I also suggested that she meet her advisor in social work. Although she did not want to talk with her advisor, she did agree that it might be worthwhile to get some input from the Sociology professor. After receiving his comments Mimi returned for an appointment.

Mimi expected that the Sociology professor would be very receptive to her proposed work, which was well supported by the US literature. Alas, she was again very disappointed by the feedback. The professor had stated that while the topic might be interesting, he could not determine her focus. He asked, 'Are you talking about the US? Somewhere else?'. He then suggested doing some comparative work so that her work would appeal to a broader audience. Like the Anthropology professor, he also urged her to 'get help with English so that her ideas would be clear'. And, like the Anthropology professor, he again focused on content and deficits in Mimi's language, as opposed to acknowledging and helping unpack the complexities of the task.

The professor's comment about language, however, reinforced Mimi's view that her writing difficulties were largely due to language, and that this was something that could be fixed in our EAP writing course and meeting with me on a regular basis. Despite the different feedback from each of the two professors, Mimi was not ready to consider the possibility that difficulties were in fact due to the forces of disciplinary differences.

Near the end of the semester, Mimi finally gave her paper to her advisor, who was aware of her interest in focusing on Korea. Thinking that she had finally sufficiently revised her paper, Mimi was again disappointed by the feedback she received. The advisor was confused, wondering what happened to Korea and whether Mimi had changed her research focus. Mimi was back to where she had started.

Some thoughts on Mimi's journey

Struggles such as Mimi's have often been attributed to cultural differences (culture here being US and Korean) and culture shock, different national rhetorics, self-imposed pressure to comply and conform, and a kind of 'genre shock' (a lack of familiarity with genre conventions). However, as a relatively new postgraduate student, a central aspect of her difficulty was that she perceived all discourse communities related to her own as homogeneous. Although a larger academic culture exists, she had not realized that disciplines need to be viewed as sub-cultures, each of which 'maintains its specific values, processes, and world views' (Reich & Reich, 2006). Unaware that different disciplines are like different cultures (Reich & Reich, 2006), Mimi had not yet realized that the feedback from the Anthropology seminar reflected the values of that discipline, particularly since each discipline 'sees itself as the centre of the universe of knowledge' (van Leeuwen, 2005), and has clear ideas as to what research might be interesting and worth pursuing. The message that Mimi took away from her first two attempts at writing her preliminary exam proposal was that her writing was bad. However, her efforts to self-initiate into different communities of practice (Wenger, 1998) almost guaranteed that she would at times 'feel fragmented, pulled in different directions, resistant, and compliant' (Casanave, 2002) and result in disappointment. Her strategy for completing the paper, while creative, left her bearing a tremendous burden.

Conflicting input was leading Mimi to increasing levels of confusion. She was at a point of crisis, which 'created a space for a strategic intervention' (Fairclough, 2005), which the two professors and, to some extent her advisor, did not recognize as an opportunity for directing a fundamental change in Mimi's thinking about her work. Mimi's journey was not an unfortunate, but necessary, part of 'the postgraduate experience', underscoring the importance of recognizing that students need to function in numerous environments, and again that our courses should equip them with the skills and strategies to do so (Hyland, 2002). This, however, poses a challenge to EAP practitioners. We know that we are not disciplinary experts and are challenged to distinguish 'those areas in need of attention that may be broadly useful within an academic milieu from those that may be subject-, area-, discipline- or even course-specific' (Swales, 1988). We are also not privy to the tacit knowledge that content professors and advisors have (Hansen, 2000), but somehow are unable to share with their students at an appropriate time. We rely on students to serve as our informants so that we can learn about the traditions in their disciplines, but often they are involved in multiple disciplines and unaware of the conventions in any of them.

The EAP literature continues to call for more research so that we have a clear picture of the exact nature of the students' textual worlds, processes of induction into their chosen disciplines, as well as the hybrid discourses and multi-modal genres they are expected to master. Because much research exists, there continues to be discussions as to how or whether EAP teachers should essentially act as proxies for content professors uninterested, unwilling, or unable to reveal to students the inner workings of their disciplines. However, I think, too, there needs to be a call for courses where these discussions would have the most impact.

Although there is still a place for general EAP classes, we need to develop advanced academic literacy courses that attract those students whose English proficiency is deemed as 'just fine' by some measure, and perhaps broaden our reach to include all postgraduate students. Such classes should not put us in the position of acting as substitutes or surrogates for content advisors; that is not our role to play. Such classes may perhaps require us to relinquish the idea that we must know in advance what our students need, and that we need to have the disciplinary content expertise before we can offer courses that achieve the level of specificity that fills the gaps in students' understanding of academic discourse. We can offer advanced classes in which students set the syllabus, which we then shape to reflect research on academic literacy, and in which we capitalize on the academic successes of our students, as suggested by Hirvela & Belcher (2001).

We have established one such course at my own institute, broadly entitled 'Dissertation Writing and Writing for Publication' (on which Mimi was enrolled). Students on the course come from a range of disciplines from the hard sciences to the humanities, thus allowing for the raising of interdisciplinary awareness. Students decide the topics for the semester based on their writing needs for the current semester, which may include typical genres such as research papers and proposals, but inevitably embody the larger goals, among others, to help students find ways to 'do things with and through language that they might not otherwise be able to do' (Turner, 2004); to draw out students' (mis) perceptions of writing; to encourage students to see the value of compiling their own corpora and that a sample size of one is not enough; and to emphasize issues of stance and engagement (Hyland, 2005) in their writing. Enrollment in the course is robust and, if this is any measure of its value, in recent years the course has been attracting increasing numbers of domestic postgraduate students (one-third of the enrollment in the current semester), despite the availability of a postgraduate writing support class offered by the university writing centre.

What was Mimi able to achieve after participating in this course? Below is an excerpt from the final draft of her preliminary examination paper submitted to her department six weeks after the course had ended.

Return to Work by Women in Korea and the US following the Birth of a Child

The central question raised in this prelim examination is what factors are associated with Korean women's return to work in the first year after childbearing. This prelim exam question is motivated by my dissertation plan to explore determinants that motivate or discourage women's return to the labor market after childbirth and, particularly, to investigate whether legislation on paid maternal leaves influences these work behaviors and decisions among young mothers in Korea.

In contrast to the limited theoretical and empirical literature on women's return to work in Korea, studies about the situation in the US are more accessible. Therefore, I decided to explore literature mainly in the US about the factors related to women's return to work after childbirth in addition to literature in Korea, so that I can broaden my knowledge and understanding about women's employment following the birth of a child. In addition, literature that examines the effects of family policies in other countries will be briefly reviewed to discuss the impacts of different elements of family policies.

> *Trends in Women's Labor Force Participation in Korea and the US*
>
> As has been well established, in both Korea and the US, women's labor force participation rates have been consistently increasing for the last several decades. Specifically, in Korea, the labor force participation rate for women aged 15–64 was 45.2% in 1985 and rose to 54.5% in 2005. In the US, labor force participation rates for women aged 15–64 increased since 1960 from 59.3% to around 70% in 2005. Despite the positive trend of increasing female participation in the labor force over time, the average participation rate in Korea is still surprisingly below those in OECD countries (60.4%), including the US (69.2%). Why is this the case?

We see that Mimi has set her own research agenda rather than borrowing one set by others. Although she did settle on a comparative focus, that was her decision. More importantly, Korea has returned. She has adopted a stance toward her research area, and is attempting to engage her reader. The question she raises is characterized as central, and her motivation is stated clearly. Mimi has also put herself back into her writing through the use of first person, and she is attempting to engage her reader by asking a question at the end.

I will not attempt to argue that any of the transformation in the writing above is due to my brilliance as an instructor. On the contrary, I think Mimi was on a journey much like the characters in *The Wizard of Oz*, who had to endure many trials and tribulations in the Land of Oz before at the end realizing that all along they had already possessed the things that they needed most. The analogy works. What she needed most was the awareness that she had her own story to tell, rather than someone else's, together with the confidence and appropriate positioning to tell it.

References

Becher T. & Trowler T. (2001). *Academic tribes and territories: intellectual enquiry and the cultures of disciplines* (2nd edn.). Philadelphia, PA: Open University Press.

Braun, T. & Schubert, A. (2007). The growth of research on inter- and multidisciplinarity in science and social science papers, 1975-2006. *Scientometrics, 73/3*, 345–351.

Casanave, C. (2002). *Writing games: Multicultural case studies of academic literacy practices in higher education*. Mahwah, NJ: Lawrence Erlbaum.

Committee on Science, Engineering, and Public Policy (2004). *Facilitating interdisciplinary research*. Washington, DC: The National Academies Press.

Fairclough, N. (2005). Critical discourse analysis in transdisciplinary research. In R. Wodack and P. Chilton (Eds.), *A new agenda in (critical) discourse analysis*. Amsterdam: John Benjamins.

Hansen, J. G. (2000). Interactional conflicts among audience, purpose, and content knowledge in the acquisition of academic literacy in an EAP course. *Written Communication, 17/1*, 27–52.

Hirvela, A. & Belcher, D. (2001). Coming back to voice: the multiple voices and identities of mature multilingual writers. *Journal of Second Language Writing, 10/1–2*, 83–106.

Hyland, K. (2000). *Disciplinary discourses Social interactions in academic writing*. London: Longman.

—— (2002). Specificity revisited: how far should we go now? *English for Specific Purposes, 21/4*, 385–395.
—— (2002). Authority and invisibility: Authorial identity in academic writing. *Journal of Pragmatics, 34/8*, 1091–1112.
—— (2005). Stance and engagement: a model of interaction in academic discourse. *Discourse Studies, 7/2*, 173–192.
Lea, M. R. & Street, B. (1999). Writing as academic literacies: understanding textual practices in higher education. In C. N. Candlin & K. Hyland (Eds.), *Writing: texts, processes and practices*. London: Longman.
O'Regan, K. & Johnston, H. (2001). We all know what an article review is ... or do we? Unpublished manuscript. University of South Australia.
Reich, S. M. & Reich, J. A. (2006). Cultural competence in interdisciplinary collaborations: a method for respecting diversity in research partnerships. *American Journal of Community Psychology, 38/1–2*, 51–62.
Reiss, R. (2000). Interdisciplinary research and your scientific career. *The Chronicle of Higher Education*. [Retrieved March 5, 2009 from http://chronicle.com/article/Interdisciplinary-Research-and/46386/].
Report of the Subcommittee on Interdisciplinarity. (1999). [Retrieved March 23, 2009 from http://www.provost.umich.edu/reports/issues_intersection/interdisciplinarity.html].
Swales, J. M. (1988). *Episodes in ESP: a source and reference book on the development of English for science and technology*. New York: Prentice Hall.
Swales, J. M. (1990). *Genre analysis*. Cambridge: Cambridge University Press.
Swales, J. M. & Feak, C. B. (2000). *English in today's research world*. Ann Arbor, MI.: University of Michigan Press.
Turner, J. (2004). Language as academic purpose. *Journal of English for Academic Purposes, 3/2*, 95–109.
van Leeuwen, T. (2005). Three models of interdisciplinarity. In R. Wodack & P. Chilton (Eds.), *A new agenda in (critical) discourse analysis*. Amsterdam: John Benjamins.
Wenger, E. (1998). *Communities of practice: learning, meaning, and identity*. Cambridge: Cambridge University Press.
Zhu, W. (2004). Faculty views on the importance of writing, the nature of academic writing, and teaching and responding to writing in the disciplines. *Journal of Second Language Writing, 13/1*, 29–48.

SECTION II

Specificity in language use

PHILIP NATHAN

MODAL VERBS IN BUSINESS CASE REPORTS

INTRODUCTION

Case studies comprise a core vehicle for teaching and learning in the field of academic business education (Easton, 1982; Maufette-Leenders et al., 1987). Linked to this core role, case studies also form an important locus of assessment on these academic business programmes, with assessment types including the writing of advisory reports based in cases, the writing of critiques analyzing and evaluating specific company actions and strategies adopted in cases, and the generation of short answer responses to specific business case-based questions.

The study presented here was based in a UK business school where students were required to write business case reports as part of their master's programme of study. Such reports were therefore of significant interest in terms of support programmes focusing on student writing in particular, as initial investigations suggested that the writing of case reports was problematic for non-native speaker (NNS) students. A particular area identified in initial studies as presenting challenges for NNS students was the accurate and appropriate deployment of modal verbs in relation to statements concerning company actions and strategies.

Although some research on case studies and case report writing had previously been conducted in the US context from an ethnographic perspective (Freedman et al., 1994; Freedman & Adam, 1996; Forman & Rymer, 1999a, 1999b), little information was available at a lower textual level considered of relevance to supporting student writing, with no information available on modes of evaluation or use of modal verbs presented in the US research, and no linguistic research identifiable on business case report writing in the UK context.

In order to provide a more solid research base for the teaching of case report writing to NNS (and NS) students, efforts were made to characterize case reports as written by students at the target business school. To this end a small corpus of 53 native and non-native speaker (mainly East Asian) business case reports written on a postgraduate marketing programme at the UK business school was constructed (ca.125,000 words). Analysis of the corpus with regard to aspects of modal verb usage and deployment is presented in this paper.

Description of the corpus and outline of the case report tasks

Tasks were derived from two component modules in the relevant postgraduate marketing programme, with approximately half written on a marketing management module and half on a module focusing on e-commerce and marketing (Table 1). E-commerce and marketing texts were written as part of a three-hour examination in which the case was pre-seen and case report writing accounted for one of three examination writing tasks. Marketing management reports were written as part of continuous assessment over several weeks and were longer; approximately 3,000 words compared to around 1,600 words for the marketing examination case reports.

Two tasks accounted for 95 per cent of the reports in the corpus: the main marketing management task (25 of the 28 continuous assessment case reports) focusing on the generation of a broad strategic plan within a specific market, with the e-commerce and marketing case task[1] (25 case reports) centred on the development of a marketing plan within the context of the 3Ps (product, price, promotion) of the marketing mix. The marketing task rubric required writers to act in the role of consultant presenting a report to senior partners in a consultancy firm. No role-play requirement was presented in the main marketing management task information.

Foci of the modal verbs[2] usage study

Modal verb occurrence was investigated in terms of overall and individual modal frequency in whole case reports, and considered in relation to speaker type and business specialism (marketing or marketing management). More detailed analysis of modal verb occurrence in options analysis elements of the case reports was conducted, incorporating specific analysis of modal verb clausal functions in these report components.

Table 1 Corpus composition

Task specialism/Speaker type	NS texts (words)	NNS texts (words)
Marketing management tasks (continuous assessment)	14 (44,286)	14 (41,523)
E-commerce and marketing task (examination)	8 (14,356)	17 (25,189)

[1] Referred to henceforth in this paper as the marketing examination case report, the concept of e-commerce not being a component of the task set.

[2] The semi-modal 'have to' is incorporated within modal verb counts in this paper.

Overall modal verb frequency data

Table 2 shows combined modal verb frequencies in the case report corpus by specialism and speaker type. Individual modal verb frequencies were determined using the *Wordsmith Tools* 3.0 analytical tool. While the data seems to suggest higher levels of modal deployment in NS case reports, and such a claim is supported by statistical analysis using the log likelihood (G^2) tool ($p < 0.05$), analysis using non-parametric Mann-Whitney U tests, which incorporate consideration of distribution between corpus text components, did not identify significant difference in total modal verb distribution between the NS and NNS sub-corpora at $p < 0.05$.

Table 2 Total modal verb frequencies by specialism and speaker type

Modal verb occurrences per thousand words	NS	NNS
Marketing management tasks (continuous assessment)	28.7	28.7
Marketing (examination)	29.9	24.4
Whole corpus	29.0	24.0

Frequencies of individual modal verbs in the case reports

A wide range of modal verbs was deployed in both marketing and marketing management task-based reports. However, there were a number of differences apparent in individual modal verb deployment raw frequencies between NS and NNS case report writers on comparison of the marketing management task case reports and the marketing examination report task data (Figures 1 and 2). As can be seen from the graphs, the extent and nature of individual modal verb deployment within the case reports also varied in relation to the specialism-based task performed.

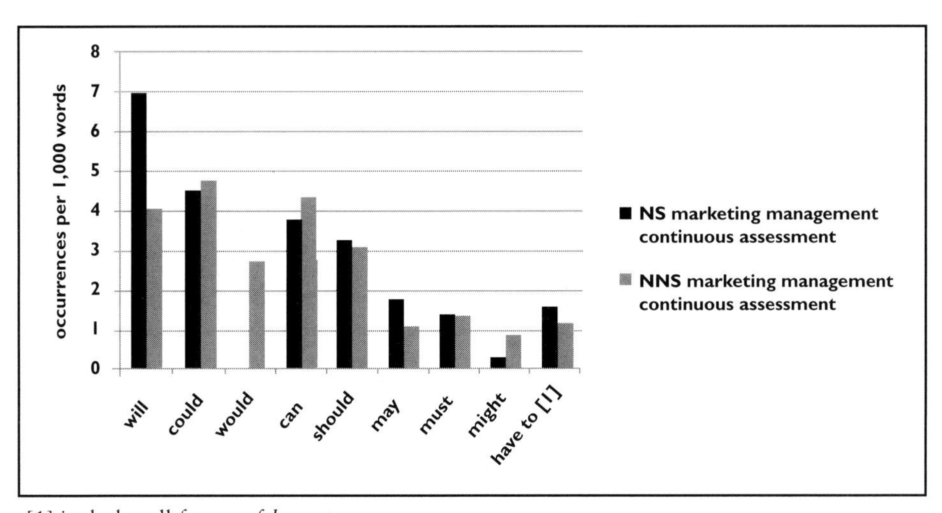

[1] includes all forms of *have to*

Figure 1 Frequencies of individual modal verbs in NS and NNS marketing management continuous assessment report texts

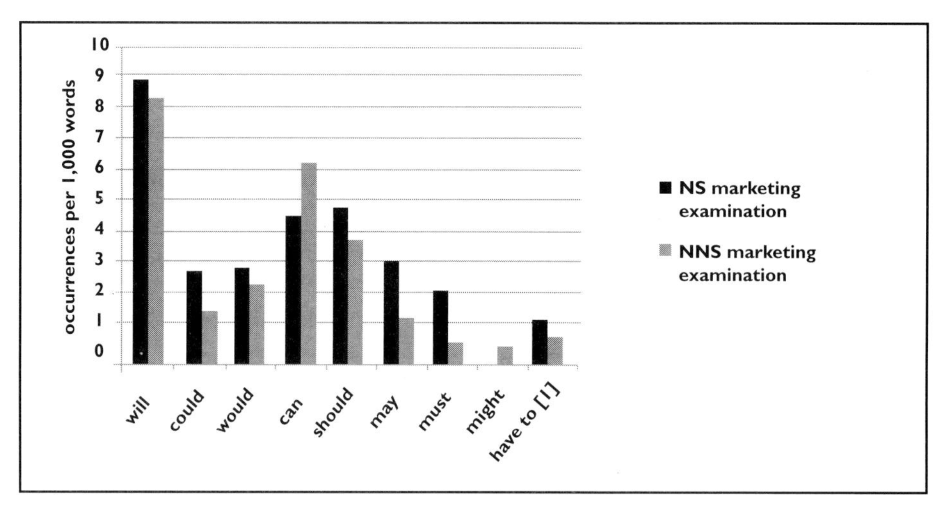

Figure 2 Frequencies of individual modal verbs in NS and NNS marketing examination task case report texts

Focusing on individual modal verb frequencies, statistical analysis using the Mann-Whitney U parameter identified only *would* as occurring at higher frequencies in NS compared to NNS reports ($p < 0.05$). However, comparison of *would* frequencies in the different text type sub-corpora, found significant frequency difference between NS-NNS samples only in the case of the marketing management reports, with no significant difference in *would* deployment between NS and NNS marketing reports. Mann-Whitney analysis identified significant differences in frequencies of the modal verbs *could*, *may* and *must*, with these modal verbs occurring at higher frequency in NS compared to NNS marketing examination reports. Comparing across report types, *would*, *could*, *have to* and *must* were found to be statistically more frequent in the NNS marketing management reports compared to the NNS marketing reports.

Clearly a range of differences in modal verb deployment is apparent. The origins of these modal verb deployment differences, identified in terms of task specialism and speaker type, are considered to lie in both the extent and nature of rhetorical features in the different case report sub-components, and the varying clausal functions performed by these modal verbs. These factors are considered in the following sections.

Distribution of modal verbs within the case reports

In terms of six broad rhetorical moves identified in these case reports, namely orientation, analysis, options and alternatives, advisory, summary and consolidation moves, and supplementary supporting information (unpublished data[3]), which incorporate the more overt structural components of the marketing and marketing management case reports, modal verb distribution appeared to be linked to the extent and frequency of these rhetorical moves, which themselves varied in frequency and extent in relation to the particular task-specialism and assessment type.
Considering modal verb distribution in terms of rhetorical moves in NS and NNS marketing examination report texts[4], 84 per

cent of modal verbs were found to be located in the advisory move which, as the name suggests, focuses on the provision of report advice and recommendations. This move comprised approximately 69 per cent of examination report text. By contrast, only 7 per cent of modal verbs occurred in options and alternatives moves comprising 6 per cent of text. In contrast, in marketing management continuous assessment texts 24 per cent of modal verbs occurred in the advisory move, comprising 19 per cent of text, while 47 per cent were found in options and alternatives moves, comprising approximately 30 per cent of report text. Variations in the frequency and extent of individual rhetorical moves between NS and NNS samples were identified, but differences could not be determined as significant given the relatively small corpus size and the consequential potential influence of individual texts on corpus data. Nevertheless, where notable differences in extent and frequency of specific moves were observed, combined modal verb counts were higher in rhetorical moves as a proportion of overall text where a particular rhetorical move was more extensive within the NS or NNS sub-corpus, and lower where the rhetorical move was less extensive. For example, the summary and consolidation move comprised approximately 6 per cent of text in marketing examination reports with 7 per cent of all modal verbs present, while the analytical move comprised 20 per cent of text, and contained 14 per cent of all modal verbs.

Individual modal verb frequencies in case report component structures

Breaking down the overall corpus and sub-corpus categories into text structural components, such as *introduction* or *problem definition,* clearly results in relatively low levels of text for analysis within each structural category and, since all text structures do not occur in all case reports, further reduces the number of texts available for analysis. Nevertheless, considering the deployment of modal verbs within each structural category does identify some interesting findings. As can be seen from Figure 3, the more hypothetical modal verbs *could* and *would* occur at notably higher frequency in sections dealing with options analysis (comprising the options and alternatives move), with the modal verbs *can, should* and *will* comparatively frequent in 4Ps[5], recommendations and STP (segmentation, targeting, positioning) sections (comprising elements of the advisory move), and also in conclusions sections (defined as comprising a summary and consolidation move).

[3] Manuscript in preparation.

[4] It is recognized that combining data in this manner could produce distortions due to interactions between speaker type and task-specialism features, however this combined data is, on balance, considered to represent a sufficiently reliable picture of modal verb distribution

[5] While the task rubric specified use of the 3Ps of product, price and promotion, the majority of writers used 4Ps, including the final P of place.

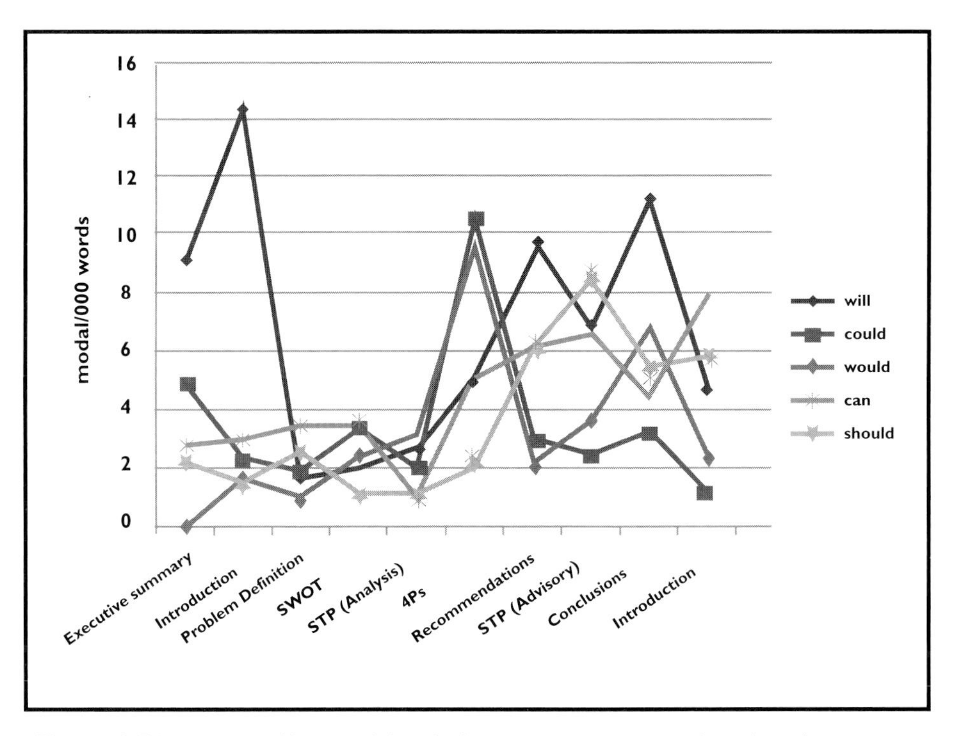

Figure 3 Distribution of key modal verbs in case report structural sections from marketing and marketing management case report texts (combined NS and NNS data)

Clearly the modal *will* is also, as might be anticipated, identified at very high levels in introduction components, but also, contrasting with expectations, *will* is found at high levels in executive summaries. Rhetorical functional analysis of executive summaries suggested significant misunderstanding, by native speakers in particular, with regard to the nature and purpose of executive summaries, with NS titled executive summaries frequently containing content more characteristic of introduction texts[6].

Differences in deployment of the modal verb *would* have been described above both in terms of speaker type and in relation to task-specialism. The deployment of this particular modal verb is therefore of some interest. Figure 4 shows the distribution of the modal verb *would* in structural sections of the marketing management case reports. The data indicates that NS writers are deploying this modal verb at higher levels in options analysis structural components compared to NNS writers, this observation being supported by log likelihood analysis[7].

[6] This observation has not been generalized to other contexts.

[7] At this level of data it becomes highly unlikely that Mann-Whitney U will generate any significant differences and therefore this statistical tool is not deployed in these cases.

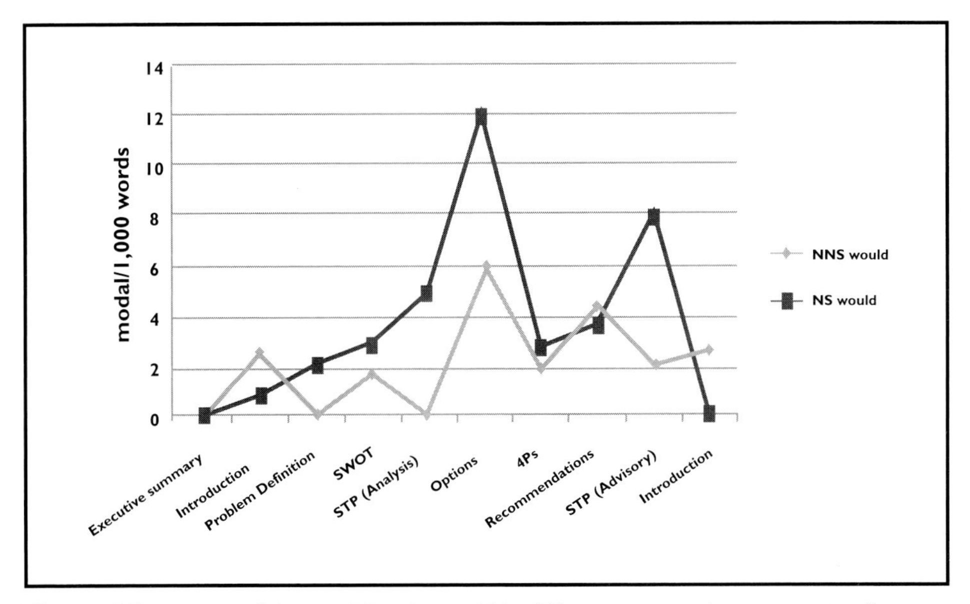

Figure 4 Frequency of the modal verb would in different structural components of marketing management continuous assessment reports

This differential NS-NNS deployment of *would* in these options analysis structural components having been identified, further investigation was conducted into the more detailed rhetorical and functional origins within the options analysis elements underpinning these differences. Differential deployment of *would* was found to be linked to the prevalence and extent of specific rhetorical moves and sub-moves in these options analysis structural elements, in particular with regard to an options implementation move and specific sub-move components within the implementation move related to 'implementation of a proposed implementation action or strategy' and 'evaluation of the implementation action or strategy'. The implementation move was found at higher frequencies in NS options analysis components (as were the relevant component sub-moves), compared to NNS structural components, with higher levels of *would* as a consequence also identified in the NS options elements.

In terms of broad meaning, the *would* modal verb was associated with the expression of hypotheticality. Detailed analysis focusing on the clausal functions supported by *would*, based in a developed set of clausal categories arising from the work of Thompson (2000, 2001), identified significant differences in the clausal functions supported by *would* in NS and NNS options components. Key differences lay in the frequent use of *would* by NS writers (24 uses) to support clauses proposing courses of action as in the following example:

> A third option would be to leave the prices as they were and branch out into HD.
>
> (sample C1E sub-section 3, move 1 sub-move 2)

Only a single example of the use of *would* to support this function was identified in NNS samples. In terms of raw frequency, within options components, *would* also supported higher levels of NS clauses stating requisite actions as in:

Budgets would need to be tightened throughout the division.

(sample C1A sub-section 1, move 3 sub-move 1)

identifying hypothetical consequences as in:

This would result in Baxter regaining its market share.

(sample C1F sub-section 3, move 4 sub-move 1)

and expressing direct evaluation as in:

This passive approach would have few advantages.

(sample C1E sub-section 1, move 1 sub-move 5)

Discussion and conclusion

Modal verbs are key linguistic components of the pedagogical business case reports analysed in this study, occurring at high frequencies as a class of verb in case reports overall, and being identified in all rhetorical moves and structural components. Patterns of modal verb deployment were found to differ according to business specialism as well as speaker type. These differences originate in differential rhetorical realisations in the different report categories and, in the case of NS-NNS differences with regard to the modal *would*, have been shown to be related to differential deployment in relation to supported clausal functions.

In relation to research on modal verbs in the areas of EAP and ESAP, while Thompson (2000, 2001) has focused on broader clausal functions of modal verbs, research which has incorporated investigation into the use of modal verbs has significantly focused on epistemic aspects of modal verb functionality concerning degrees of author commitment to propositional statements (for example Hyland & Milton, 1997; McEnery & Kifle, 2002). The rhetorical contexts in which modal verbs operate have not been significantly scrutinised.

While the current study is based on a relatively small corpus and a small number of case report tasks, the data analyzed supports the notion that differences in frequency of modal verb deployment in different contexts by different speaker groups (NS-NNS) are likely to be grounded in varying rhetorical structure and text realisations, and clausal functionality, in addition to factors such as grammatical function and epistemic commitment.

With regard to pedagogy, developing learner awareness of the key role of modal verbs within the context of business case reports would seem a valuable pedagogical practice. Examination of the uses of *would* within these reports for the expression of hypotheticality, and in particular for expression of specific clausal and rhetorical functions, would seem of significant value.

REFERENCES

Easton, G. (1982). *Learning from case studies*. London: Prentice Hall International.

Forman, J. & Rymer, J. (1999a). Defining the genre of the 'case write-up'. *Journal of Business Communication, 36*, 103–133.

Forman, J. & Rymer, J. (1999b). The genre system of the Harvard case method. *Journal of Business and Technical Communication, 13*, 373–400.

Freedman, A., Adam, C. & Smart, G. (1994). Wearing suits to class: Simulating genres and simulations as genre. *Written Communication, 11*, 193–226.

Freedman, A. V. & Adam, C. (1996). Learning to write professionally: 'Situated learning' and the transition from university to professional discourse. *Journal of Business and Technical Communication, 10*, 395–427.

Hyland, K. & Milton, J. (1997). Qualification and certainty in L1 and L2 students' writing. *Journal of Second Language Writing, 6*, 183–205.

Maufette-Leenders, L. A., Erskine, J. A. & Leenders, M. R. (1997). *Learning with cases*. London, Ontario: Richard Ivey School of Business, University of Western Ontario.

McEnery, T. & Kifle, N. A. (2002). Epistemic modality in essays of second language writers. In J. Flowerdew (Ed.), *Academic Discourse*. Edinburgh: Longman.

Thompson, P. (2000). Modal verbs in academic writing. In B. Ketteman & G. Marko (Eds.), *Language and computers: Teaching and learning by doing corpus analysis. Proceedings of the fourth international conference on teaching and language corpora*. Graz: Rodopi.

Thompson, P. (2001). Academic writers: Putting modal verbs to work. In G. Aston & L. Barnard (Eds.), *Corpora in the description and teaching of English: Papers from the 5th ESSE conference (Helsinki) Bologna CLUEB*, (pp. 25–43).

David D. Qian and Yongyan Li

Specificity in clusters: profiling the discourse of the financial services industry in Hong Kong

Introduction

The issue of specificity has been foregrounded in ESAP (English for Specific Academic Purposes) in recent years. While the idea of 'different strokes for different folks' (Hyland, 2002:389) is easy to grasp, ESAP practitioners are faced with a specific group of students who would still earnestly welcome the availability of a repertoire of language facts that are gleaned from the students' target academic or professional communities.

With students that aim to enter the financial services industry for example, apart from using such textbooks as *English for Banking Studies* (McLisky, 2008) and *Absolute Financial English* (Pratten, 2009), they may well also take the advantage of derivations from a corpus of texts compiled from their target workplaces. To quote Aston (2002:9), 'home-made' corpora are appropriate for learning purposes because they can be 'specifically targeted to the learners' knowledge and concerns'. Indeed, there has been a growing interest in exploring the phraseology of specialized home-made corpora for teaching and learning purposes over the years, which has been a main theme in corpus-based pedagogy (Bowker & Pearson, 2002; Lee & Swales, 2006). Nevertheless, it seems fair to say that research tends to overtake classroom applications and, meanwhile, many more corpus-based studies have been published on the phraseology of academic discourse (e.g., textbooks, student essays, classroom speeches), than of professional discourse, or discourse produced in professional contexts.

In this paper we will illuminate the notion of specificity by focusing on 'clusters', or high-frequency repeated word sequences in a specialized corpus, namely Hong Kong Financial Services Corpus (HKFSC). In doing so, we will demonstrate features of clusters that are bound to specific text types, while exemplifying a method that ESAP professionals can replicate to explore the specificity in their own home-made corpora.

LITERATURE BACKGROUND

The focus of our interest, 'clusters', has been called 'recurrent word-combinations' (Altenberg, 1998), 'n-grams' (Forchini & Murphy, 2008), and 'chains' (Stubbs & Barth, 2003) in the literature, but are perhaps best known as 'lexical bundles' (hereafter LBs) (Biber et al., 1999; Cortes, 2004; Hyland, 2008). In our study we use the term 'clusters' throughout, to refer to sequences such as *in terms of (the), (in) (the) first half (of), at the latest (predicable date)* as well as *requires your immediate attention*. It is thus important to point out that our definition of 'clusters' is somewhat different from that for LBs in the literature, where LBs are commonly defined on the basis of two empirical criteria, i.e., the cutoff point (e.g., 20 per million, as in Cortes, 2002) and scope of occurrence (e.g., occurrence in at least 10 per cent of texts, as in Hyland, 2008); with the application of such criteria, many LBs are structurally incomplete (e.g., *in terms of the*). A more exclusive definition of LBs, as exemplified by Simpson (2004), is to include only those expressions with 'structural and idiomatic coherence' (ibid. 42), thus *in terms of* and *I think that* are called LBs, while *in terms of the* and *you know what I* are not, the argument being that semantically complete expressions are learnt more easily than those that are not.

Our definition of clusters echoes the less exclusionary definition of LBs. However, while previous researchers have generally focused on four-word LBs, in our study we do not constrain ourselves within this territory. Instead, for example, we combine sequences like *continue to be, continue to, will continue to, continues to, continued to* into *(will) continue to (be)*, which we then call 'clusters', and the occurrence of which in the corpus is a sum of the occurrence of each of the foregoing five strings. Underlying our pattern-like kind of definition of clusters in the study is a pedagogically-driven rationale: firstly, in our specialized corpus, clusters are highly various, but they can normally be defined in terms of a stem element (e.g., *continue to*) plus grammatical variations around the stem; secondly, including two-word units (e.g., *continues to*) is in congruence with Sinclair's (2002) observation that excluding two-word units, which are apparently the most frequent word units in English, is a misrepresentation of the prevalence of multi-word units in the language; and finally, from a pedagogical point of view, looking beyond four-word clusters seems justified in a specialized corpus, even though such clusters are likely to be relatively few.

Previous researchers have also studied high-frequency LBs in functional terms. Functional taxonomies for LBs have been suggested and a correspondence between the functional categories of LBs (e.g., referential bundles, text organizers, stance and interactional bundles) and Halliday's (1994) description of linguistic functions is described (Biber et al., 2004; Cortes, 2004). It is useful to note, however, as Hyland

(2008) demonstrates, that adjustment to a relatively broadly-defined functional taxonomy may be necessary as genre varies. LBs in research articles, for instance, fall into 'the three broad foci of research, text and participants, and introduces sub-categories which specifically reflect the concerns of research writing' (ibid. 13).

Overall, in the literature there is still no clear picture as to the use of clusters (in our definition) within specific domains of communication, illuminating the nature of high-frequency clusters as well as their functions. Hyland (2002:385) has rightly pointed out 'ESP must involve teaching the literacy skills which are appropriate to the purposes and understandings of particular academic and professional communities'. Through an investigation into high-frequency clusters in a specialized corpus, we highlight the notion of specificity and aim to generate pedagogical insights.

Our study

We had two research goals in the study: 1) to identify high-frequency clusters in the Hong Kong Financial Services Corpus (HKFSC), and 2) to explore how clusters may vary across text types in the corpus. The corpus under interrogation in this study was HKFSC, a comprehensive reservoir of the written discourse in the financial services industry in Hong Kong. The HKFSC was compiled by the Research Centre for Professional Communication in English in the Department of English, The Hong Kong Polytechnic University. The corpus contains 25 text types, such as annual reports, brochure, fund description, ordinances and speeches. Two computer programmes used in this study were *WordSmith Tools* (Scott, 2008), and *Range* (Nation & Heatley, 2007), which is available as a free downloadable zip file at www.vuw.ac.nz/lals/staff/paul-nation/nation.aspx

For the first research goal, i.e., identifying high-frequency clusters in the HKFSC, the steps followed were: a) running the cluster function of *WordSmith* (setting the search at two-word and above); b) selecting those with an occurrence of 40 per million or above (which means setting the cutoff point at 275 occurrences, with the given size of the corpus, i.e., around 6.8 million tokens; c) excluding those clusters that are persons' names or proper nouns, and those that we consider have little pedagogical value (e.g., *in Hong Kong, of the group, would like to, any of, last year, its subsidiaries, due to*); and d) tabulating clusters.

For the second research goal, i.e., exploring how clusters may vary across the different text types of the corpus, we focused on examining: a) how four-word clusters diverge in a few selected text types; b) how several keywords enter into different clusters and display different semantic properties across text types; and c) how some clusters are bound to certain functional stages found in particular text types.

Results and discussion

High-frequency clusters in the HKFSC

Following the steps delineated above, a total of 352 clusters was obtained, which can be broadly classified into around ten structural categories. The three structural categories that contain the most clusters are the following: *a/the N of (the) (N)*, with 67

Table 1 High-frequency clusters in the HKFSC

Clusters	Concurrent Distinct Words
(is/are/as) set out (in) (the) (appendix/note/below)	investment management/objective/portfolio/properties/securities
(the) stock exchange (of)	consolidated balance sheet/financial statements/profit and loss
in respect of (the/any/which)	dividends share/price
in accordance with (the)	executive director(s)/officer
(for) the year (ended)	are/be/is required to
pursuant to (the)	the terms of (the)
(in) (the) first half (of)	(as) (at) the latest practicable date
for the purpose(s) (of)	for further enquiries please contact
(at) the end of (the)	with effect from
(the) fair value(s) (of)	where applicable

(19.03 per cent) clusters/patterns, *Adj+N* with 65 (18.47 per cent) clusters/patterns, and *N+N* with 48 (13.64 per cent) clusters/patterns. Table 1 shows a collection of high-frequency clusters in our corpus, although they do not necessarily feature these top three structural categories.

When checked with the computer programme *Range*, the 352 clusters/patterns feature altogether 1,151 running words (tokens) and 447 distinct words (types). Twenty of the distinct words occurring five times or more (indicated below by parenthesized numbers) in the selected clusters/patterns are the following:

assets, date (10)
value (9)
year (7)
account, number, securities, share (6)
amount, balance, capital, company, director, income, information, liabilities, loss, management, sheet, total (5).

In terms of their ranking in the wordlist of the whole corpus, these 20 words range from No.22 (*company*) to No.314 (*sheet*), with a mean ranking of No.102. Considering that many of the top-ranking words in the corpus are grammatical words, it seems the content words that appear in high-frequency clusters are also of relatively high-frequency in the whole corpus.

Variation of clusters across text types

Here we present a few lines of evidence to demonstrate variations of clusters across text types in our corpus.

a) There is only limited overlap between frequent four-word clusters in a few selected text types.

To delimit the scope of investigation, we checked four-word clusters in the following three text types in the HKFSC:

Annual reports (<800,000 tokens)
Media release (>560,000 tokens)
Speeches (<610,000 tokens).

Table 2 From the top-50 clusters containing *financial* across three text types

Annual Report	Media Release	Speeches
the **financial** statements	**financial** protection products	international **financial** centre
the **financial** year	the **financial** secretary	Asian **financial** crisis
derivative **financial** instruments	principal **financial** group	the **financial** secretary
financial reporting standards	major **financial** centres	international **financial** architecture
financial risk management	financial services company	the **financial** crisis
personal **financial** services		the **financial** services

It was found that in the top 100 of the four-word clusters in each of the three text types, only one cluster is shared, which is *at the end of* (+time). The saliency of this cluster coincides with Forchini and Murphy's (2008) report that this same sequence is the most frequent sequence in a corpus of financial newspapers. Meanwhile, in terms of the four-word clusters, the gap between the three text types in our corpus is apparently even bigger than that found by Hyland (2008) across four disciplines, where five LBs are shared across the most frequent 50 four-word LBs across the disciplines. This can be regarded as an indicator for the linguistic variation between the three text types.

b) Keywords enter into different clusters and display distinctive semantic prosodies in a text type.

We examined how a number of keywords in the HKFSC (with the British National Corpus as the reference corpus) enter into clusters across text types. Table 2 presents the clusters containing one of the keywords, *financial*. The given clusters were taken from the top 50 clusters in each of the three text types noted above, i.e., annual reports, media release, and speeches. As Table 2 indicates, overlap across the text types is again limited (with the overlapping elements shown in bold in the table).

It has been shown that keywords in business texts display certain semantic features (Nelson, 2006). Table 3 shows the *semantic prosodies* of the word *financial* in frequent clusters within the text type of speeches. Stubbs's (1995:255) definition of *semantic prosody* is adopted here:

'A semantic prosody is a linguistic relation between a node word and a lexical set. This relation is defined by a very general semantic feature (for example, 'unpleasant'), or by a more specific semantic field (for example, 'care') whose members are established from corpus data.'

The contrast shown in Table 3 seems to indicate that the dominant semantic prosodies around a certain keyword may be linked to both the *aboutness* of the text (Cheng, 2007) and the ideological positioning and rhetorical strategies of the speaker (Partington and Morley, 2004).

Table 3 Frequent clusters (with *financial*) in speeches and semantic prosodies

Frequent cluster	Semantic prosody
Asian/the financial crisis Asian/the financial turmoil	'problem'
leading financial centre international financial community	'locale'
international/global/our financial system our financial infrastructure	'system'
financial liberalization effective international financial intermediation	'action'

c) Some clusters correspond to particular functional 'stages', which have enriched the variation of clusters across text types.

As indicated in Table 4, across text types a range of high-frequency clusters can be identified, each of which corresponds to a functional 'stage' (Martin, 1984), manifesting the communicative purpose of the text type concerned.

Table 4 Clusters across text types and the corresponding stages

Text type (with tokens)	Cluster	Freq. per million	Stage	Example
Fund report (359,137)	It is intended that the investments will be	557	To state investment objective	'It is intended that the investments will be made on a diversified basis.'
Investment description (1,426,951)	the occurrence of a qualifying event	131	To state provision of guarantee	'The qualifying period in respect of a member may also be re-set to zero if the member (or his personal representative) effects a redemption, switching out or withdrawal of the units of the fund other than upon the occurrence of a qualifying event.'
Circular (372,489)	requires your immediate attention	97	To call for attention	'This circular is important and requires your immediate attention.'
Prospectus (1,746,262)	please refer to the paragraph headed	92	To signal cross-referencing	'For further details of the supply of our raw materials, please refer to the paragraph headed "Raw Materials, Fuel and Utilities" in the "Business" section.'
Speeches (607,729)	I look forward to	64	To close on goodwill	'...I look forward to greeting a stronger financial industry, imbued with an even stronger sense of fairness and justice to all, which seeks to prosper in the commercial life of this great community of ours.'
Corporate announcement (382,023)	Hong Kong limited takes no responsibility for the contents	34	To disclaim	'The Stock Exchange of Hong Kong Limited takes no responsibility for the contents of this announcement, makes no representation as to its accuracy or completeness...'

Previous research has suggested that 'clusters recur because they are key structuring devices which are register- (or genre-) sensitive' (McCarthy & Handford, 2004:176). Table 4 seems to indicate that the involvement of some clusters in constructing the functional stages of a text type is a factor contributing to the variation of clusters across text types.

Conclusion

In this paper we reported a pedagogically-driven study where we aimed to arrive at a collection of high-frequency clusters in the Hong Kong Financial Services Corpus (HKFSC), and to find out to what extent the text types in the corpus display varied use of clusters. For the first aim, we identified 352 highly-frequent clusters in the corpus; for the second aim, we found that frequent four-word clusters diverge quite drastically across text types, that keywords are embedded in different clusters with varied semantic prosodies, and that some clusters correspond to particular functional stages which make up specific text types. Pedagogically, this would mean that high-frequency clusters can make a reasonable starting point of learning for students aiming to grasp the language of a specialized community, as due attention to the variation of the clusters across text types in terms of their connection with key words, semantic prosody and function will help to hone students' specialized 'literacy skills' (Hyland, 2002). Finally, what we have shown in this paper exemplifies what ESAP (English for Specific Academic Purposes) professionals can do to explore the specificity in their own classroom corpora.

References

Altenberg, B. (1998). On the phraseology of spoken English: The evidence of recurrent word combinations. In A. Cowie (Ed.), *Phraseology: theory, analysis and applications*, (pp. 101–122). Oxford: Oxford University Press.

Aston, G. (2002). The learner as corpus designer. In B. Kettemann & G. Marko (Eds.), *Teaching and learning by doing corpus analysis: proceedings of the Fourth International Conference on Teaching and Language Corpora*, (pp. 9–25), Graz 19–24 July, 2000. Amsterdam & New York: Rodopi.

Biber, D., Conrad, S., & Cortes, V. (2004). If you look at ...: Lexical bundles in university teaching and textbooks. *Applied Linguistics*, *25*, 371–405.

Biber, D., Johansson S., Leech G., Conrad S., & Finegan E. (1999). *Longman grammar of spoken and written English*. Harlow: Longman.

Bowker, L, & Pearson, J. (2002). *Working with specialized language: A practical guide to using corpora*. London: Routledge.

Cheng, W. (2007). Concgramming: A corpus-driven approach to learning the phraseology of discipline-specific texts. *CORELL: Computer Resources for Language Learning*, *1*, 22–35.

Cortes, V. (2002). Lexical bundles in freshman composition. In R. Reppen, S. M. Fitzmaurice, M. & B. Biber (Eds.), *Using corpora to explore linguistic variation*, (pp. 131–145). Amsterdam & Philadelphia: John Benjamins.

— (2004) Lexical bundles in published and student disciplinary writing: Examples from history and biology. *English for Specific Purposes*, *23*, 397–423.

Forchini, P., & Murphy, A. (2008). N-grams in comparable specialized corpora: Perspectives on phraseology, translation, and pedagogy. *International Journal of Corpus Linguistics*, *73(3)*, 351–367.

Halliday, M. A. K. (1994). *An introduction to functional grammar*. London: E. Arnold.

Hyland, K. (2002). Specificity revisited: How far should we go now? *English for Specific Purposes, 21*, 385-395.
— (2008) 'As can be seen: Lexical bundles and disciplinary variation.' *English for Specific Purposes, 27*, 4–21.
Lee, D., & Swales, J. (2006). A corpus-based EAP course for NNS doctoral students: Moving from available specialized corpora to self-compiled corpora. *English for Specific Purposes, 25*, 56–75.
Martin J. R. (1984). Language, register and genre. In F. Christie (Ed.), *Language studies: Children writing*. Geelong: Deakin University Press.
McCarthy, M. & Handford, M. (2004) 'Invisible to us': a preliminary corpus-based study of spoken business English. In U. Connor & T. A. Upton (Eds.), *Discourse in the professions: Perspectives from corpus linguistics* (pp. 167–201). Amsterdam/Philadelphia: John Benjamins.
McLisky, M. (2008). *English for banking studies*. Reading: Garnet Publishing.
Nation, P. & Heatley, A. (2007). 'Range.' Retrieved from http://www.vuw.ac.nz/lals/staff/paul-nation/nation.aspx
Nelson, M. (2006). Semantic associations in business English: A corpus-based analysis. *English for Specific Purposes, 25*, 217–234.
Partington, A. & Morley, J. (2004). At the heart of ideology: Word and cluster/bundle frequency in political debate. In B. Lewandowska-Tomaszczyk (Ed.), *Practical applications in language and computers* (PALC 2003), (pp. 179–192). Berlin: Peter Lang.
Pratten, J. (2009). *Absolute financial English*. Peaslake, UK: Delta Publishing.
Scott, M. (2008). *WordSmith Tools (version 5.0)*. Oxford: Oxford University Press.
Simpson, R. C. (2004). Stylistic features of academic speech: The role of formulaic expressions. In U. Connor & T.A. Upton (Eds.), *Discourse in the professions: Perspectives from corpus linguistics*, (pp. 37–64). Amsterdam/Philadelphia: John Benjamins.
Sinclair, J. McH. (2002) Review. *International Journal of Corpus Linguistics, 6/2*, 339–359.
Stubbs, M. (1995). Corpus evidence for norms of lexical collocation. In G. Cook & B. Seidlhofer (Eds.), *Principles and practice in applied linguistics*, (pp. 245–256). Oxford: Oxford University Press.
Stubbs, M. & Barth, I. (2003). Using recurrent phrases as text-type discriminators: A quantitative method and some findings. *Functions of Language, 10/1*, 61–104.

Mary Davis and John Morley

The role of reusable phrases in postgraduate writing: multidimensional perspectives

Introduction

In the context of academic writing for international students within UK universities, one of the most common instructions for assignments tends to be 'use your own words', and that 'plagiarism must be avoided'. Yet these simplistic warnings ignore the fact that the words we use are actually shared, as are many of the recurrent phrases we can find in written texts. While native writers may be quick to recognize commonly used multi-word sequences, sense when they may be recycled in their own writing from another text without risk of accusations of plagiarism, and manipulate them creatively through substituting, adding or subtracting some elements, it is unclear how well non-native writers can do this. In this study, we firstly set out to ascertain whether or how far non-native students at pre-Master's level could recognize, re-use and be creative[1] with reusable phrases, and then, as a second stage, to examine postgraduate students' understanding of the role and use of recurrent phrases in their own writing. As a follow-up, to complement these investigations, we sought the views of a small number of experienced practitioners about the role of reusable phrases in academic writing and on the desirability of giving this important area some attention on an EAP writing syllabus.

Theoretical background

Our starting point for this work is the premise that much of the language that we produce is phraseological in nature. That is, as well as being able to produce new constructions from combining different elements according to a set of rules, we are also able to learn, retrieve and produce whole sequences as phrasal chunks. Early insights into this phenomenon included those of Firth (1951), who introduced the term 'collocation', and Bolinger (1976), who argued that the rule-governed basis of language was actually over-emphasized, and that much of the language we produce is repetitive and not particularly creative. Later empirical findings, derived from the use of large electronic corpora and concordance

[1] Creative: an ability to incorporate new or different linguistic elements into phrases.

software, appear to have since supported Bolinger's claims. For example, based on his experience directing the Collins Cobuild project, Sinclair (1991) suggested that, while grammar enables combinatorial possibilities, in reality much of what is produced consists of semi-preconstructed phrases.

Sinclair's observations have been supported by many other corpus studies, which show that much of spoken and written language is formulaic in nature (e.g., Baayen & Lieber, 1991; Altenberg, 1993), comprising a high number of semi-preconstructed phrases. Certain forms of written communication, such as academic writing, seem to be particularly rich in phraseological constructions (Nattinger & DeCarrico, 1992; Hyland, 2008). A writer's display of a good range of commonly used phrases, together with the subject-specific terminology, may be another way of illustrating a degree of mastery within their discipline. The use of familiar phraseology may also be a way for a writer to establish a common ground with his or her audience, as other members of their discourse community. Importantly, research has also shown that there is a much greater incidence of non-standard phraseology in non-native speaker writing, reflecting a general lack of awareness of preferred phraseological structures (Howarth, 1998). Even if they have a well-developed knowledge of English grammar and vocabulary, non-native users of English often still tend to have a restricted repertoire of phraseological constructions.

This fact has been recognized within the field of EAP, and many practitioners acknowledge that helping learners notice useful multiword expressions in academic texts adds a valuable dimension to EAP pedagogy. One well-known EAP textbook, for example, gives the following advice:

> ... borrowing the words and phrases of others can be a useful language learning strategy. Certainly, you would not be plagiarizing if you borrowed items that are commonly or frequently used in academic English. (Swales and Feak, 2004:172)

The assumption here is that such phrases are common property and that, once identified, they can be 'borrowed' and reused by other writers – in this case non-native speaker students. This may be termed 'manifest intertextuality' (Fairclough, 1992), where the use of elements from other texts is very clear in a new text. The particular example given to students in the textbook referred to above is: *The results from this experiment seem to suggest that ...* (ibid. 172). This type of phrasal construction has been termed a 'sentence builder' by Nattinger & DeCarrico (1992:165), since it provides a framework for a complete sentence, and it also allows for the possibility of variation. In fact, this is only one of the numerous descriptive terms found in the literature, including 'learned sequences and ready-made phrases' (Goldman-Eisler, 1964), 'prefabricated routines' (Brown, 1968), 'prefabricated pattern' (Hakuta, 1974) and 'lexicalized stems' (Pawley & Syder, 1983). For our purposes, however, we adopted the term 'reusable phrase', because it is very simple for students to understand and because it makes explicit its reusable nature.

There is evidence that many international students bring to their academic writing differing understandings of the complex issues involved in textual borrowing (Pennycook, 1996). We felt that promoting the use of 'reusable phrases' in writing to this group might present some interesting challenges, and we wanted to examine how well our students were able to do this. This stage of our work is described in the section that follows.

Stage One

In the initial stage of this research, our aim was to examine the ability of pre-Master's students (in different disciplines) to recognize reusable phrases, then to re-use them and be creative in their use. The research was undertaken with 23 mainly East Asian students on an EAP course at Oxford Brookes University. Students were given a text at the beginning and end of the semester, and were asked to highlight any phrases they thought were re-usable for academic writing, having been given some examples such as 'there are three main reasons for this' (different texts were given to control for any text-related effects). This was contrasted with the recognition of phrases made by native speaker experts (five EAP tutors). Surprisingly, we found a high level of recognition in the first attempt by students, with some of the recyclable phrases identified by the experts being recognized by up to 86 per cent of students. As a result, little evidence of any development of recognition in the second attempt was detected.

During the semester, five stages of teaching input on re-usable phrases were given using *Academic Phrasebank*[2] *(AP)* (Morley, 2005). Rather than present listed phrases in isolation, an effort was made to engage students in meaningful awareness-raising and understanding of the use of these phrases, through tasks involving identifying word forms and replaceable components, constructing sentences, completing cloze texts and discussing the rhetorical moves (Swales, 1990) in the categorization of *AP*, such as 'Reporting Results'. The individual use of these phrases was then examined in the final submissions by the students of a 3,000-word assignment at the end of the module. It was found that 30 per cent of students employed more than 40 recyclable phrases in their texts, especially at the beginning of sentences, with a mean of 31 phrases (thus approximately 3–4 per cent of the text) for the whole group. An additional finding was that there was a high degree of correlation between the grades that students achieved and the mean number of phrases they were using ($rho = 0.889$, $n = 23$, $p < .0005$, two-way, Spearman). For example, the mean number of phrases for the group achieving an A grade was 49, while that of the group achieving a C grade was 18.5.

The last part of the investigation at this stage was to examine evidence of creativity in students' use of phrases. We found examples of phrase use which looked unusual, and to verify our results used the search engine Google to indicate how common these combinations might be, thus using a strategy widely used by academics to check language (Mottley, 2004). Where there were few hits for phrasal combinations, we classified them as creative. However, analysis was only carried out with a small number of instances; no systematic analysis of creativity was possible at the textual level, since we could only identify this where non-typical word combinations were present.

At the end of stage one, it was felt that further research was needed to explore how students would transfer their exposure to phrases on this EAP course into their postgraduate study. This developed the rationale for stage two.

Stage two

In this stage, we wanted to examine these postgraduate students' understanding of the role and use of recurrent phrases in their own writing, and to look at the decisions they made when using phrases. We interviewed 5 from the original 23 students six months later, when they had started their postgraduate course and had already completed an assignment. The first part focused on a discussion of participants' use of these phrases in their assignment. The second part of the interview involved a discussion of their perceptions of the role of phrases. The participants studied Sports Nutrition (A), Built Environment (B), Finance (C) and Law (D and E).

[2] *Academic Phrasebank* is a free, online, generic resource which lists a wide range of typically used academic phrases.

Reviewing their own assignments, participants (A, B, C, D and E below) were first asked where they took the phrases from, why they used them in the position they did, and whether they considered them to be creative. Examples of phrases they used include:

A: 'On the same note but at the other end of the scale ...'
B: 'It can be easily found from the figure above ...'
C: 'This population is regarded as a potential opportunity for ...'
D: 'To start the research, it is important to clarify the terms ...'
E: 'Currently it is becoming increasingly difficult to ignore ...'

The sources for these phrases were given as: class, an IELTS book, a grammar book, an academic article and *AP*. The reasons for use included that students felt them 'to fit'; they made the information stand out or look more academic. Some felt they were creative, for example, in the combination of one phrase with another.

Participants went on to discuss the role of phrases in their writing. They considered them to be important in different ways:

A: 'I can design sentences with them so they make sense and look better.'
B: 'They help me think and to start my work.'
C: 'I need to make sure what I write is academic. If I don't use these phrases, it cannot be called academic.'
D: 'I can refer to key ideas with these words as a link between me and the reader.'
E: 'Without these phrases, the essay is too simple.'

These very enlightening responses indicate that participants found a range of possible roles for phrases in sentence building, as a cognitive tool to promote thought, as a tool for establishing a communicative 'link' with the reader, or in order to adhere to the perceived stylistic norms of their prospective discourse community.

We also asked about how the participants saw the difference between these phrases and those needing to be referenced; they saw the reusable phrases as being 'general', or 'not specific, or belonging to an individual'. Taking this a step further, we enquired whether these phrases could ever become plagiarism; the response was only if they were 'connected to a specific idea, not on their own'. These responses indicated a clear distinction for the students between re-usable phrases and plagiarism. They gave the following answers to further questions: how much they used the phrases (either 'a lot' or 'not enough'), whether they felt they were creative ('sometimes'), how they collected and learnt phrases (most popularly, 'using notebooks'), and how they put them into their writing (often through 'categorizing', and 'having certain phrases ready for different sections'). These comments seem to show that they were making use of their learning in stage one.

Stage three

In the final stage of the project, we sought to obtain the insights and views of a small number of expert informants. The rationale for incorporating this element of our work arose from the fact that, at the original presentation at the conference in Reading, in which we reported on stages one and two, we found our paper generated considerable interest, evident in thought-provoking questions from the audience. It struck us that a useful adjunct to student views on phrases would be the views of experienced practitioners who were informed about the area of academic phraseology. Four members of the audience, all known to the researchers, were identified as being expert informants and agreed to be interviewed.

[3] A list of the informants and their current professional activities is included in the Appendix.

Thus, the third stage seemed to be a natural extension of the work we were already undertaking[3]. In the interviews, our informants were asked to comment on the role of recurrent phrases in academic writing, their preferred pedagogic approaches to this area, and the dangers and benefits coverage of this area may present to students.

Firstly, each informant recognized the very important role played by phrases in academic writing. One commented that this was 'much bigger ... than anyone ... even people, who think about language, would recognize' (MW). Another informant suggested that there was something inevitable about their presence in academic text:

> 'They are obviously important, in fact they are inevitable I would suggest. I don't think that anybody can read academic prose or write academic prose without coming across these kinds of standardized phrases.' (JSw)

Although the importance was thus acknowledged by all our informants, the pedagogic approaches suggested were somewhat diverse, ranging from explicit tutor-led selection and modelling approaches to strategies that were primarily concerned with encouraging students to learn to identify and analyze useful phrases in relevant academic texts, working on their own. To encourage discipline specificity in phrasal use, one informant, for example, explained how he asked his students to identify reusable phrases in a corpus composed of the 'favourite' journals in their field and to compare the patterns of use in the corpus with the way they used the phrases in their own writing. All our informants agreed that studying the phrases within their broader context was essential.

Our informants gave insights on the possible dangers associated with this area. Two informants suggested that there was a danger students might acquire competence in manipulating useful pre-formulated phrases, but fail to engage in the content and meaning at a deeper intellectual level, thus stunting creativity (JSl and MW). In some cases, it was acknowledged that this could lead to plagiarism issues (MW). Another danger mentioned was a possible risk of overwhelming students, and perhaps undermining their motivation, by introducing them to the vast range of linguistic possibilities and collocational combinations which exist at the phraseological level (MA). Of course, the fact that the vast range exists can sometimes result in students using 'convoluted, artificial and quite odd phraseology' (JSw). Despite these concerns, all informants found benefits in raising students' phraseological awareness. One informant suggested that it could help students to sound like they belong to their academic community (MW). Another argued that it facilitates a wider area of available language for students to be more able to express themselves (JSl). Lastly, two others felt that phrases served as 'crutches' (JSw) or 'pegs' (MA) to help students get started in their development of ideas and in their writing, or even to get their ideas to 'flow'.

Conclusion

The study has provided some perspectives on the role of re-usable phrases in academic writing at pre-Master's and Master's level, using views of a small number of students and experts. The first stage explored pre-Master's students' ability to recognize, re-use and be creative with recurrent phrases. The students showed high levels of recognition, and a correlation was found between their ability to use phrases and their results for the academic writing module. Some examples seemed to show creativity, although this was difficult to assess. The second stage indicated that the students had a good understanding of the role and usefulness of reusable phrases. While they saw the function of re-usable phrases in various ways, including sentence-building, as a cognitive tool, a communicative method, and an essential component of academic writing, they all recognized their importance. This coincided with the views of experts explored in the final stage. The informants considered it essential to raise awareness about these phrases, and to do so within given contexts, using varying pedagogical approaches. Coverage of this area in EAP courses is therefore recommended. The researchers recognize the limitations of this small-scale study and suggest further research on developing discipline-specific areas of phrasal use.

REFERENCES

Altenberg, B. (1993). Recurrent verb complementation constructions in the London-Lund Corpus. In J. Aarts, P. de Hann and N. Oostdijk (Eds.), *English Language Corpora: Design, Analysis and Exploitation*, (pp. 227–245). Amsterdam: Rodopi.

Baayen, H., & Lieber, R. (1991). Productivity and English derivation: a corpus based study. *Linguistics*, *29*, 801–843.

Bolinger, D. (1976). Meaning and Memory. *Forum Linguisticum*, *1*, 1–14.

Brown, R. (1968). The development of wh-questions in child speech. *Journal of Verbal Learning and Verbal Behavior*, *7*, 279–290.

Fairclough, N. (1992). *Discourse and social change*. Cambridge: Polity Press.

Firth, J. R. (1951). Modes of Meaning. *Papers in Linguistics, 1934–51*, (pp. 190–215). Oxford University Press.

Goldman-Eisler, F. (1964). Discussion and further comments. In E. Lenneberg, (Ed.), *New Directions in the Study of Language*. Cambridge, MA: MIT Press.

Hakuta, K. (1974). Prefabricated patterns and the emergence of structure in second language Acquisition. *Language Learning*, *24/2*, 287–298.

Howarth, P. (1998). Phraseology and Second Language Proficiency. *Applied Linguistics*, *19/1*, 24–44.

Hyland, K. (2008). Academic clusters: text patterning in published and postgraduate writing. *International Journal of Applied Linguistics*, *18/1*, 41–63.

Morley, J. (2005). Academic Phrasebank. Retrieved from www.phrasebank.manchester.ac.uk

Mottley, J. (2004). Is Google suitable for detecting plagiarism? *LTSN Bioscience Bulletin*, *12 (6)*. Retrieved from ftp://www.bioscience.heacademy.ac.uk/newsletters/ltsn12.pdf

Nattinger, J. & DeCarrico, J. (1992). *Lexical phrases and language teaching*. Oxford: Oxford University Press.

Pawley, A., & Syder, H. (1983). Two puzzles for linguistic theory: Nativelike selection and native like fluency. In J. C. Richards & R. W. Schmidt, (Eds.), *Language And Communication*, (pp. 191–225). New York: Longman.

Pennycook, A. (1996). Borrowing others' words: Text, ownership, memory and plagiarism. *TESOL Quarterly*, *30/2*, 201–230.

Sinclair, J. (1991). *Corpus, concordance, collocation*. Oxford: Oxford University Press.

Swales, J. (1990). *Genre analysis: English in academic and research settings*. Cambridge: Cambridge University Press.

Swales, J. & Feak, C. (2004). *Academic Writing for Graduate Students*. Ann Arbor: University of Michigan Press.

Appendix

Our four informants were: John Slaght (Assessment Co-ordinator and Course Director, Centre for Applied Language Studies at University of Reading); Melinda Whong (Lecturer in Applied Linguistics, Language Centre at Leeds University and BALEAP Research Officer); Mary Anne Ansell (Executive Director of Language Centre at Leeds University); and John Swales (Professor of Linguistics, University of Michigan).

SECTION III

Specificity and course design

Benet Vincent and Müjde Sener Nordling

Researching and implementing a pedagogical genre: the short answer

Introduction

Learners' future academic success depends on their ability to write according to the conventions of academic writing on faculty courses (Johns, 1997). This paper reports on the implementation of short answer examination questions into an EAP programme following research carried out into faculty writing. The introduction of short answers was seen as an important step in meeting the academic needs of the learners and facilitating their successful integration into university life.

Background information about the institution

The medium of instruction at Sabanci University (SU) is English. All undergraduates are required to take the SU English Language Assessment Exam (ELAE). Learners who pass this exam become freshmen while those who do not meet the standards of English language proficiency are placed in one of three levels of English instruction in the Foundation Development Year (FDY) programme in the School of Languages (SL). The FDY course has certain key features.

- FDY courses are not purely exam-based. Advancement from one level to another is based primarily on fulfilling the course requirements. Examinations are only a portion of these requirements.
- The coursebook used, *Beyond the Boundaries* (Dobie et al., 2003), was produced and published in-house. It is a three level content-based course designed specifically for learners on the FDY programme.
- In addition to developing learners' English language proficiency and academic skills, this approach helps them to expand their knowledge of the world, both past

and present, and to identify various relationships between events.

There are around 60 teachers in the SL from Turkey, Britain, America, South Africa and Australia who are experienced in a range of academic teaching contexts.

In their freshman year, learners take compulsory university courses which aim to equip them with interdisciplinary skills. Amongst these obligatory courses are Humanity and Society, Science and Nature and Advanced English. Second year faculty courses (e.g., Mathematics and Economics) are introductory level courses providing a general understanding to familiarize learners with the degree programmes of each faculty.

Research project overview and findings

The Writing Task Group (WTG) was set up to establish core principles of teaching writing at the School of Languages, according to instructors' views and collated data from faculty members. These would then be used to identify academic writing needs of undergraduate learners and thus to improve the writing programme accordingly and to recommend areas of materials exploitation and further development, as well as teacher training where needed.

Generally, the type of writing output learners produce in Turkish high schools is narrative and/or for grammar practice, so most learners are not familiar with the conventions of academic writing before they come to the SL. At the time the research was carried out, there was only one writing task-type implemented on the programme, the American-style five-paragraph essay, which was taught in a relatively formulaic way using a stepwise 'process approach'. Some of the assignments were based on sources, but the criteria were felt by some to be biased towards form over content. This had the effect that students who knew the format could get a passing grade in assignments for work even if their writing contained few ideas or irrelevant points.

It was felt that, if changes were going to be made to the writing syllabus, these had to 'belong' to the teachers in the SL. Therefore, it was essential that we find out what views are inherent in the SL instructors' approach to teaching/learning writing in EAP contexts, i.e., the culture of writing. Focus group interviews were held to identify what instructors felt were the core principles of teaching academic writing and what texts learners should be expected to produce during their study in the SL. Most instructors felt that students should be studying and writing the types of texts that they will be writing in faculty; this was not felt to be reflected in the writing programme at that time.

The WTG then contacted faculty members in the core subjects, asking them to provide samples of written work completed by learners who take their courses, as well as information about proportions of the grades of courses that were attributable to written work and how much of this writing was produced under examination conditions. This data was examined in detail to identify assignment types, key prompt types and linguistic features common to various disciplines, as these would have implications for the writing syllabus and guide us in terms of the types of tasks and linguistic input we may need to introduce in our writing programme. A comprehensive range of assignments and exam question types from Freshman English, Natural Sciences, Social and Political Sciences, Humanities, and Faculty of Engineering and Natural Sciences were analyzed. Findings indicated that:

- learners perform a variety of academic writing tasks in their courses, including essays and short answers written under examination conditions as well as take-home assignments of varying lengths
- the majority of their tasks will require writing from sources such as required readings, lectures or data
- more than a quarter of the writing on faculty courses consisted of examination-based 'short answers', that is, those that take up less than a quarter of a page

These findings of the types of writing undertaken by students in faculty courses contrasted with the writing experiences of students both at high school and on the FDY programme. The last of these findings seemed to represent the most pressing need for change to the programme at the time, which explains our decision to focus on introducing short answers as an assessed task.

Short answers: key features

The short answer is a type of writing that did not form part of the FDY programme at the time the research was conducted. In order to introduce the short answer into the writing programme, it was essential to define its key features. While doing so, it was helpful to envisage the short answer as a 'genre', that is a piece of writing that is given a name by parties interested in its production (Moore & Morton, 2005), while bearing in mind Johns' (2008) warning that such 'pedagogical genres', which include the essay, are more loosely defined and less closely studied since they have a lower status than other more prestigious academic genres and consequently are more liable to variation across disciplines.

An invaluable tool in the task of categorizing types of short answer was Horowitz's typology of essay examination questions, which he derived from analysis of prompts submitted to him by faculty at Western Illinois University (Horowitz, 1986). This typology categorizes university examination prompts according to the type of knowledge they require learners to demonstrate; this has implications for the rhetorical function that an effective response will employ. Table 1 sets out the four general types established by Horowitz (ibid).

In summary, short answers, one of the most common types of university examination writing in our context, vary in length from one sentence to several sentences and usually require the use of one type of communicative function: either definition (Type I), comparison, or describing a cause or an effect (Type II), or a description of a process (Type III), although longer types may involve combinations of these. It is also worth mentioning that *Type IV: familiarity with argumentation* was not a function associated with short answer questions, no doubt because they typically involve 'reproduction of information' from sources covered during a course (Moore & Morton, 2005).

Table 1 Horowitz's typology (1986) with examples

Type	Asks learner to demonstrate	Type of writing involved in response	Examples of prompts
Type I	familiarity with a concept	a definition, description or explanation	Define *Bolshevism*
Type II	familiarity with the relations among concepts	comparison, explanation of cause-effect relationship, or a classification	Compare *Communism* and *Fascism* What are the causes/effects of species diversification? Classify three different types of political system.
Type III	familiarity with a process	description of a historical or technical process	Describe the process by which you would treat a patient with a lymphoma. Outline the rise of Fascism in Germany and Italy.
Type IV	familiarity with argumentation formulating or reporting an argument	Summarise the arguments for/against free trade.	Fukuyama says we have reached the end of history. Do you agree?

Implementing the findings in teaching and assessment

Once the main features of short answers had been established through analysis of prompts and samples provided by faculty using the typology set out in Table 1, it was necessary to work out how to put these into practice. Certain principles were established to try to ensure that the transition to teaching of what was effectively a new pedagogical genre would be as smooth as possible; they are explained below.

When introducing a new pedagogical genre such as the short answer, it is only natural that there should be an element of apprehension amongst instructors at the thought of entering unfamiliar territory. It was therefore an important principle that instructors should have as much information and guidance as possible about changes. To this end an Academic Writing Guidelines (AWG) booklet (Dobie et al., 2007) was produced which set out the features of short answers and included ideas for introducing them in class, based on the core course materials. Such ideas were also discussed and worked on in workshops provided for instructors, some of which were run by our consultant on the project, Ann Johns.

This implies the second principle, which was that all short answer work should be based around the textbooks used in the school already, *Beyond the Boundaries* (Dobie et al., 2003). One of the findings of the research into faculty writing reported above was that a large majority of student writing in faculty is based on sources. This means that learners need to be content responsible; their writing should accurately reflect what they have read or heard. It was therefore decided that instructors in their level teams should note the important topics covered in the textbooks, which then would form a pool on which examination questions could be based. Guidance was provided by the assessment team, who suggested that certain criteria should be used to ensure that topics are well chosen:

- Coverage – topics chosen should be covered in sufficient depth in core materials to be worth devoting time to learning.

- Surrender value – as far as possible, topics chosen should reflect learners' future needs in faculty courses.
- Gradability – topics chosen should be sufficiently well defined in the core materials that it is possible to test knowledge of them.

These 'topic lists' are now set out in syllabus documents so that both instructors and learners are fully aware of important course content.

A further, text-based principle was that writing teaching should be based on models of the types of pattern that learners were expected to write so that their attention could be drawn to the language of realization of such patterns. Since the textbooks used in the FDY were produced in-house and reflect the academic needs of our learners, this was a relatively easy task. A fairly straightforward example of a frequently found pattern is 'concept-class-characteristics', or CCC for short, which is used for definitions and was first brought to our attention by Ann Johns. An example taken from the Academic Writing Guidelines booklet (Dobie et al., 2007) is shown in Figure 1.

Concept	**Class**	**Characteristics**
a telescope	*is an instrument*	*that magnifies distant objects*
a 'kına gecesi	*is a party*	*given by the bride shortly before she gets married and attended only by female friends & relatives*

Figure 1 The CCC pattern

Once again, the various rhetorical patterns that learners are expected to learn are explicitly stated in syllabus documents which are available to all stakeholders.

Analysis of rhetorical patterns was felt to go hand in hand with prompt analysis training for learners, since prompts contain important information that is often overlooked, including clear indications of the type of answer expected, the length expected, the number of items to be covered and even what should not be included, which is referred to as 'proscription' by Horowitz (1986). It is also helpful in that learners' attention can be drawn to the fact that certain words, such as 'discuss', may have different meanings in different questions (Dudley-Evans, 1986).

Practical issues

The practical applications of these principles have led to the development of what are termed 'content quizzes' based on the topics for a given unit, which are intended to encourage learners to review and revise content studied on a regular basis and develop their awareness of the need for content responsibility. Such quizzes include items aiming to develop learners' recognition skills, for example by matching prompts to answers or writing prompts based on a given answer, as well as items that focus on production of short answers. They are also intended to be integrated into the teaching of writing by giving learners feedback on how they can improve their writing. A more recent development has also been to use a process approach to short answers, giving learners a chance to redraft answers written in class on the basis of teacher feedback focusing on language, task fulfilment and rhetorical pattern.

It should also be acknowledged, however, that the introduction of a new pedagogical genre into a teaching programme is not a straightforward process;

it requires a high level of motivation on the part of the instructors involved and also needs to be carefully staged so that instructors are gradually encouraged to leave their comfort zone. Where possible, features of writing that are common both to existing tasks and the new tasks should be emphasized. In our case, this was quite difficult, since the existing approach involving formulaic five-paragraph essay writing had underemphasized content and had given less importance to rhetorical flexibility. Thus, the adoption of short answer writing, in which students are expected to be content responsible, involved changing instructor perceptions of what is valued in writing. Despite stakeholder input throughout the process to ensure that all those involved were aware of what was happening and the rationale for changes proposed, we faced several practical challenges. These included lengthy discussions related to the extent to which students are expected to 'memorize' content, whether the source texts had enough depth of content and whether the content covered was relevant. Such issues were addressed as noted above by taking into account 'coverage' and 'surrender value' of topics covered. Training sessions and piloting of tasks also helped to overcome these challenges.

Assessment criteria

The criteria used to assess short answers written under examination conditions (see Figure 2) have been developed in collaboration with the assessment team on our programme and are based on the research findings as well as the practicalities of implementing short answers set out above. 'Task fulfilment' was an obvious choice to reflect the increased focus on content responsibility in the programme and the fact that learners are now encouraged to view texts more as vehicles of information than as linguistic objects (Johns & Davies, 1983). 'Rhetorical pattern' likewise matches the emphasis we now place on encouraging learners to increase the coherence and, indeed, the cohesion of the texts they write. It should also be pointed out that, since the criteria match closely the way that the short answers are taught in class, they are very easy to use.

1. **Use of language** – the degree to which the answer is clear because of the range and accuracy of the language.
   - range and accuracy of grammar
   - range and accuracy of vocabulary
2. **Task fulfilment** – content: the amount and the accuracy of the information in responding to the prompt.
   - completeness of response
   - accuracy of response
3. **Rhetorical pattern** – language of/the use of appropriate rhetorical patterns/structures.
   - degree of coherence of the rhetorical pattern
   - the accuracy of use of language of the rhetorical pattern

Figure 2 Short answer assessment criteria

Conclusion

It is clear from the foregoing that we feel that the introduction of short answers has brought a number of benefits with it. Amongst these are that learners are increasingly aware of the need to become more rhetorically flexible (Johns, 1997), that is, to vary their writing to suit various situational factors. There is also the advantage of providing more variety to writing teaching. Moreover, these changes have raised the profile of writing on the programme, as well as the level of debate about writing and what features of writing the programme values. Finally, there is the satisfaction of knowing that the writing instruction that learners are now getting is more in line with their needs when they move into faculty. Such benefits make the hard work involved in introducing this new task type worthwhile.

It should be mentioned, however, that it remains to be demonstrated that these changes are making a significant difference in terms of the quality of learner examination performance in faculty and whether this is perceived by both learners and faculty members as having an impact. This could be the focus of future research, as could investigations into the efficacy of using a process approach to improve learner writing of examination genres.

REFERENCES

Dobie, G., Einer, J., Garinger, D., Mustafa, A., & Yanova, M.Y. (2003). *Beyond the Boundaries: English in an Academic Environment.* Istanbul: Sabanci University.

Dobie, G., Hazell-Yildirim, A., Şener, M., & Vincent, B. (2007). *Academic Writing Guidelines.* Unpublished booklet.

Dudley-Evans, T. (1986). A consideration of the meaning of "discuss" in examination questions. In P. Robinson, (Ed.), *Academic writing: Process and product.* ELT document (pp. 129, 47–52). Hong Kong: Modern English Publications.

Horowitz, D. (1986). Essay examination prompts and the teaching of academic writing. *English for Specific Purposes*, *5/2*, 107–120.

Johns, A. (1997). *Text, role and context.* New York: Cambridge University Press.

Johns, A. (2008). Genre awareness for the novice academic student: an ongoing quest. *Language Teaching*, *41/2*, 237–252.

Johns, T. & Davies, F. (1983). Text as a vehicle for information: the classroom use of written texts. *Reading in a Foreign Language*, *1/1*, 1–19.

Moore, T. & Morton, J. (2005). Dimensions of difference: a comparison of university writing and IELTS writing. *Journal of English for Academic Purposes*, *4/1*, 43–66.

Sarah Horrod

Authenticity and complexity of task: still a role for ESAP?

Introduction

Diversity is a feature of taught postgraduate programmes. Some are pure or research oriented, many are applied and can be described as 'semi-vocational programmes that recruit students from a variety of disciplines' (Deem & Lucas, 2006:3). Marketing is one such discipline that attracts international students interested in the practical application of knowledge and skills. Although an MA such as Marketing has a strong theoretical element, many of the assignments and exams reflect the practical application, which results in a wide variety of task types, often including real-world elements such as writing a report for a marketing manager, as well as the necessity to demonstrate depth of marketing knowledge. Therefore, such tasks in an academic setting are, by their nature, semi-authentic. Dovey (2006:394) has described these tasks, which exhibit a mix of academic and professional elements, as 'hybrid' tasks.

This paper will investigate this increasing tendency towards 'hybrid' tasks (ibid. 394), the challenges it poses for students and how EAP teachers can respond to this trend effectively. Despite the variety of target assessments which might lead some to argue for a more general EAP approach, it will be suggested here that specificity of EAP modules is motivating for students. Firstly, such modules can address the very specific demands of the varied and complex tasks that a student will face in their immediate course. Secondly, with the English modules reflecting the mix of the academic and professional apparent in the subject modules, such students are further motivated by the professional element.

The issue of complexity

There is the emerging theme of complexity of tasks in universities. Dovey (ibid. 399) presents a spectrum from 'Traditional disciplines' to 'Newly vocationalized courses' in which the latter involve 'hybrid' assessment tasks. These are assessments which involve the students in both demonstrating they have acquired a body of knowledge and can apply it, and also engaging in real-world tasks such as writing a report for a particular organization, or group problem-solving followed by a presentation to interested parties. She goes on to point out that such complexity can lead to difficulty for students in interpreting correctly the demands of the task and that perhaps the best EAP teachers can do is to 'promote in students a metacognitive awareness of the way in which the structure of texts and linguistic strategies vary in relation to different purposes and audiences' (ibid. 397). Dovey (ibid. 391) further argues that in this new context, with its emphasis on transferability of skills such as 'learning how to learn' and communication skills, a narrow emphasis on specific text types or genres is inadequate as a basis for EAP classes.

This move towards the practical and professional does seem to be an increasingly widespread phenomenon and most British universities, such as Kingston, have adopted a 'skills framework' outlining key 'academic and employability' skills to be developed while studying.[1] In terms of assisting international students, this could bring together two branches of ESP; namely EOP and EAP, in an unprecedented way. Flowerdew (2005) reports on a successful English course which combines the two, developed partly as a result of student feedback expressing the wish for more professional-type tasks. A key element entails writing a report on a real-life problem facing the local community. This trend presents a challenge to the academic focus of much English teaching to international students in universities. However, in contrast to Dovey (ibid.), it is also argued here that enabling students to cope with such complex tasks in their main course requires the EAP modules to reflect and provide practice in skills and tasks specific to these complex assessment types.

The issue of specificity

Many articles have addressed the issue of 'specificity' and whether English for General Academic Purposes (EGAP) or English for Specific Academic Purposes (ESAP) is preferable (e.g., Spack, 1988; Hyland, 2002). There is undoubtedly still validity in addressing more generic tasks such as a 'report', a 'literature review' or a 'reflective' piece of writing in, for example, a mixed class, as mentioned by Hyland (2002). In this situation, in order to satisfy students' desire for 'personal relevance', students have to bring their own assignments, and comparisons take place in order to sensitize them to potential differences in, e.g., a report (Hyland, 2002:393).

In English classes supporting a particular programme, the scope for specificity is much greater and so more specific, immediately relevant, tasks seem to motivate students to attend the English classes better. Particular main course assignments can be effectively deconstructed and explained to the students and then students given the linguistic and discourse means to write an effective piece themselves (as in Feez, 2002, cited by Flowerdew, 2005:141). With the addition of challenging English assessment tasks, students can practise useful skills as well as become

[1] Also mentioned with reference to the University of Derby by Ganobcsik-Williams, A. (2006).

familiar with the nature of target texts. With such specificity, students can immediately transfer the skills learnt in the EAP classes to their subject module assignments. This is the approach taken on the compulsory EAP modules on the MA Marketing with English programme, designed for students with IELTS 6 rather than 7. With between five and eight hours of English classes per week, it is possible to use subject-specific materials and address the particular demands of many of the Marketing assignments.

METHOD

This section will explain how the English modules attempt to support the Marketing modules. It will also outline some preliminary research conducted with Marketing lecturers and students designed to investigate a) the nature of specificity, including within a discipline, b) the reasons for inclusion of hybrid tasks by subject lecturers, and c) the effectiveness of ESAP activities in preparing students for these hybrid tasks. In particular, the research aimed to find answers to the following:

Q1. What similarities and differences do Marketing lecturers perceive between different Marketing subjects?

Q2. Why are Marketing lecturers choosing to do complex or 'hybrid' tasks for assessment? What are lecturers' expectations of student writing in these assessments?

Q3. How do students perceive these tasks? What difficulties do they encounter?

Q4. How do students perceive the effectiveness of the English modules in preparing them for their Marketing assessments?

Firstly, there is an indication of how the EAP modules, in terms of their class activities and their own assessments, aim to respond to the demands of the Marketing assignments by considering one example Marketing module assessment.

Table 1 The links between one Marketing module and the EAP module

Marketing Communications Assessment 2	EAP activities and assessment
Three elements: literature review, discussion assessment and in-class test: • 'expert-novice' discussion assessment over three weeks: students present journal articles on topics and discuss practice scenarios orally • literature review on choice of three topics; take final draft to test • test: unseen short scenario, writing a memo to Marketing Director making recommendations on topic of literature review, supporting suggestions with ideas from literature	Activities: • critical literature reviews; students present work-in-progress on ideas in literature in class • test writing including looking at previous student scripts; practice of a previous year's marketing scenario in test writing conditions • memo and report writing Assessment Formative assignment: • literature review on English assignment topic Summative assignment: • report on Kingston Business School, including making recommendations • discussion assessment over two weeks, students critically evaluate journal article on topic of report • presentation on report findings

As Table 1 indicates, the English classes and assessments cover relevant text types such as literature reviews, memos and reports, and how to adapt some of these to academic and professional audiences. In fact, the second semester has a professional skills element with press releases, e-mails, pitches and negotiating also covered. English classes practise skills such as presenting a critical evaluation of journal articles, discussion skills and timed writing. The Marketing assessment is explicitly considered by students reporting on their work-in-progress on their Marketing literature review and the timed writing practice of a previous year's marketing scenario. In addition, the English assessment itself contains a mix of professional and academic elements. For instance, the report on Kingston Business School is required to have a theoretical basis, but it also has a professional orientation with its emphasis on analysis and recommendations. The students put themselves in the position of consultant, reporting on their findings by means of a written report and presentation.

Some research was conducted to seek answers to the questions above. Firstly, an online survey was developed to determine subject lecturers' perceptions of students' weaknesses and their perception of the EAP modules, but also to gather their views on their own specialism. Four lecturers completed the survey. This was followed by one-to-one interviews with three Marketing lecturers and eight students. The interviews were recorded and transcribed manually. Finally, one Marketing lecturer was interviewed again specifically to ask her to reflect on the test in the table above, primarily because of the 'hybrid' nature of the assignment. In the interview reflection, a range of test scripts was provided and the lecturer talked about why she had given those marks.

Results

Q1. What similarities and differences do Marketing lecturers perceive between different Marketing subjects?

In the questionnaires, marketing lecturers point to some key skills required in Marketing such as 'analytical strength', 'excellence in communication skills' and 'presenting and supporting a clear argument'. However, they also make comments about their own specialism. For example, Marketing Communications, in addition to an understanding of the literature and an ability to apply it to real cases, requires data gathering and both critical and creative thinking. Buyer Behaviour has been described as 'a narrow but deep area of enquiry', not using cases, which requires critical analysis of the research with little weight given to personal opinion. Global Marketing Management covers a large number of topics, requires an ability to critically analyze the associated literature and structure a clear argument, and makes extensive use of case studies. In summary, although analysis is a feature of all the sub-disciplines, some subjects have an overtly practical orientation requiring creativity, while others focus on research findings only.

Q2. Why are Marketing lecturers choosing to do complex or 'hybrid' tasks for assessment? What are lecturers' expectations of student writing in these assessments?

The Marketing Communications in-class test is the focus of this question. In the first one-to-one interview with this lecturer, she stated that students liked the practical nature of the module and its assessments. Her perception was that skills such as gathering and critically evaluating information involved in writing a literature review were skills that were equally important in their future marketing careers. As regards the test, 'it sorts out the people who can take theory and apply it rather than just write a good essay'. In terms of assessing the task, in the second reflection interview, she stated that it was about demonstrating understanding of key issues in a particular context, making justified recommendations in a focused way. She mentioned common traps that students fall into: not considering the specific scenario and just repeating the literature review, or only making recommendations with no justification or reference back to ideas in the literature. She stated that style and language were not major issues although the style of the top student, which was formal overall but used 'I' and 'we' and written in memo style, would 'work in a professional context'. One point I raised involved referencing. Another lecturer had mentioned that referencing ideas from the literature was not necessary, but this lecturer had told students they could if they wished. She reflected that the top student would have still got a distinction if they had not put in references, but the mark would not have been so high. Referencing, even though mostly in end brackets, allowed the lecturer to see quickly and clearly what the student had taken from the literature. In summary, the lecturer clearly believed that this type of assessment would replicate tasks and skills useful in their future careers, but her comments also demonstrate the need for students to use their theoretical knowledge and follow academic conventions.

Q3. How do students perceive these tasks? What difficulties do they encounter?

Students expressed satisfaction with the more practically-oriented tasks, but they did find exam writing challenging. It became clear that many students were not aware of the level of detail required or the need to present a critically evaluated and supported argument within an exam context. One student stated: 'I thought I'd written a good answer but when I got it back I was shocked at the mark. The comments said I didn't include enough detail'. With this specific test, students were confused about issues such as referencing, style and how to use the literature without just repeating it. They became aware that it was a semi-authentic task, but were unsure about how to do it effectively.

Q4. How do students perceive the effectiveness of the English modules in preparing them for their Marketing assessments?

As indicated in the table, the English classes and assessments covered many of the skills and associated language needed in the Marketing assessment and, in terms of the test, some time was spent discussing how to avoid a poor answer as mentioned above. We discussed what was authentic in terms of it being a professional-type task and what was inauthentic because of the need to demonstrate academic knowledge. We also looked at sample answers. Subsequently, students reported feeling more confident about doing the test, and those who attended these classes performed better than those who did not. One student interviewed stated: 'Now I know I have to support my ideas with the literature. I have to apply what I know'. In the interviews, most students also stated that the English classes supported most of the Marketing modules very well; two students could not think of anything more the English modules could have done to help with the Marketing assessments. Others suggested spending more time on timed writing practice. Additionally, all students interviewed reported enjoying the time spent on professional English skills in the second semester, and some would have liked more classes on this aspect.

Discussion

In terms of specificity, it seems that, although all Marketing subjects share some characteristics, there are differences in emphasis between them, and I would argue that it is worth addressing the particular demands of individual assessments. From the lecturer comments about referencing in the test, it might be argued that differences in opinion between lecturers in the same subject mean that EAP teachers cannot hope to deliver the correct message to students, and should, therefore, keep their teaching quite general. It is undoubtedly worth communicating the basic idea to students that they must always consider their audience, including the specific lecturer they are producing work for. EAP classes should, in addition, attempt to deal with the demands of particular task types, even if they are complex, because this seems to be what students value.

The 'hybrid' or semi-authentic tasks are a challenge for students and EAP teachers. However, it should be remembered that, in subjects like Marketing, students expect and enjoy the subjects and tasks where they can clearly perceive a practical element. Students are often surprised by the heavy theoretical load that exists in Marketing, but making an explicit link with the workplace helps them to see the value of the skills they are using to arrive at the written products required of them. It is true, as Dovey (2006:395) states, that: 'student writing often demonstrates a consciousness of the need to display theoretical knowledge that would not normally be included in real workplace writing'. However, discussing with students what is authentic and what is not and how to combine the two can help them deal better with such tasks. By also providing English assessments which include skills such as group discussion, presentations, critical thinking and report writing – which are not only expected in their Marketing assessments but are useful in the workplace – students are more motivated because they can see immediate but also long-term benefits.

Many of the features of 'newly-vocationalized courses' Dovey (ibid. 399) mentions can be seen in the Marketing programme described here, but what is not yet true is that 'reading and writing are incidental to the learning that takes place in performance' (ibid. 400). Students are still judged primarily by written products rather than their ability in face-to-face communication and we need, therefore, to help them with these. The emphasis is not on reproducing static texts or utterances, unchanging in format or language, but rather on the skills of adapting linguistic resources in writing or speaking in the light of the particular 'audiences and purposes' of the communication (as mentioned by Dovey, ibid. 397). For example, the writing of emails to known or unknown recipients, the difference in tone of solicited or unsolicited reports[2], negotiating with peers or negotiating with a company can all be considered. Some of these tasks will help students communicate better on their course, many will help them with their immediate assignments and some will also help them in the workplace. Such developments represent a challenge for EAP teachers, but given sufficient cooperation and resources it is an interesting challenge – familiar to those with experience of teaching ESAP.

References

Deem, R. & Lucas, L. (2006). Learning about research: exploring the learning and teaching/research relationship amongst practitioners studying in higher education. *Teaching in Higher Education, 11/1*, 1–18.

Dovey, T. (2006). What purposes specifically? Re-thinking purposes and specificity in the context of the "new vocationalism". *English for Specific Purposes, 25*, 387–402.

Flowerdew, L. (2005). Integrating traditional and critical approaches to syllabus design: the "what", the "how" and the "why?". *Journal of English for Academic Purposes, 4*, 135–147.

Ganobcsik-Williams, A. (2006). Building an Academic Writing Programme from within a discipline. In L. Ganobcsik-Williams, (ed.) *Teaching Academic Writing in UK Higher Education* (pp. 98–109). Basingstoke: Palgrave Macmillan.

Hyland, K. (2002). Specificity revisited: how far should we go now? *English for Specific Purposes, 21*, 385–395.

Spack, R. (1988). Initialising ESL students into the academic discourse community: how far should we go? *TESOL Quarterly, 22/1*, 29–52.

Yeung, L. (2007). In search of commonalities: Some linguistic and rhetorical features of business reports as a genre. *English for Specific Purposes, 26*, 156–179.

Andy Gillett and Angela Hammond

Pre-Master's course design: what can we learn from assessment?

Introduction

This paper presents a discussion of a model for course design of a pre-Master's programme that adopts an innovative approach to assessment. Its analysis of assessment practice is based on original data that was gathered as part of an internally funded research project the authors carried out in their institution, and demonstrates the importance of bringing assessment into the early design stages of any course (Moon, 2002).

The University of Hertfordshire has run a successful International Bridging Programme for ten years. The purpose of this generic two-semester programme was to prepare students to embark on courses in higher education at postgraduate level. It accepted students from a wide range of subjects, combining students from backgrounds as diverse as Art and Design, Mechanical Engineering and Law. The programme was devised to allow for these disciplinary differences but no more than that.

The ethos of the programme was that in order to succeed in postgraduate education, mastery of subject content cannot be achieved without developing competence in communication and study skills. As these competences and skills are partly developed and evidenced through the assessment process, the task of helping students to handle assessment was central to its design. Because of the wide range of subjects, the programme concentrated on general postgraduate skills and language and was assessed mainly through essays, reports and oral presentations.

When the programme became due for revalidation, it was felt that a new direction was needed, with a name change and a reduction from two semesters to one. At the end of 2008, we started designing the International pre-Master's Programme. Data from an earlier study (Gillett & Hammond, 2009) was used to consider the kind of assessment tasks postgraduate students have to deal with and tailor the new programme to disciplinary differences as fully as possible.

Background to assessment

While it is clear that there are innumerable examples of good and innovative assessment across the Higher Education sector, there is still concern that as a tool for learning it is too reliant on practices that are rooted in the past and lacking in flexibility. Criticisms are often made that assessment (e.g., Brown, 2004; Knight, 2002):

- is too traditional in its approach
- is not tailored to the learner
- denies the learner the opportunity to develop strategies for future learning or to take responsibility for their learning
- is not imaginative enough in the methods it uses
- fails to make sufficient use of feedback or formative assessment tools

In short, the sector does not build enough on good practice informed by, for example, the work of Rust (2002). An approach based on constructive alignment (Biggs, 2003), where the student is able to construct meaning only when teaching methods and assessment tasks line up with learning activities and outcomes, too often remains the ideal rather than reality. Rather than being 'fit for purpose' (Brown, 2004) and fit for the twenty-first century, assessment practices frequently appear to be those that have worked in the past (Biggs, 2003) or always been used (Rowntree, 1987).

Assessment is required to keep pace with 'a society committed to learning through life' (Dearing, 1997) and to allow the learner to be placed at the heart of the process, able to benefit from a supportive and structured framework through sustained use of formative assessment (Sadler, 1998). We knew this to be the case and set about constructing our new pre-Master's programme to respect this ethos.

Methodology

As the main objective of our new programme was to prepare students for Master's programmes in a wide range of disciplines, we returned to our original research to determine the nature of assessment tasks that took place at this level across our institution. As before, we used three guiding principles on the design of assessment. These were: the need to consider the cognitive dimension of any assessment task (Biggs, 2003); the need to take into account the specific nature of each task (Habeshaw, Gibbs & Habeshaw, 1993); and the need to ensure a suitable fit between the assessment method and its purpose (Rowntree, 1987). The hierarchy of intellectual development outlined in Bloom's Taxonomy of Educational Objectives (Bloom, 1956) was also influential at this stage of our research.

In our original research we had sampled all the modules at our institution and investigated the types of assessment tasks that the students would be involved in. We separated these tasks into:

1. Tasks that called for *interaction* between learners. This focuses on learner engagement and allows for innovative practice to be identified.
2. Tasks that asked for learning to be *represented* though another medium than the written word.
3. Tasks that emphasised learner *participation*. The learner is required to engage in the process and to be part of a contractual process wherever the learning takes place.

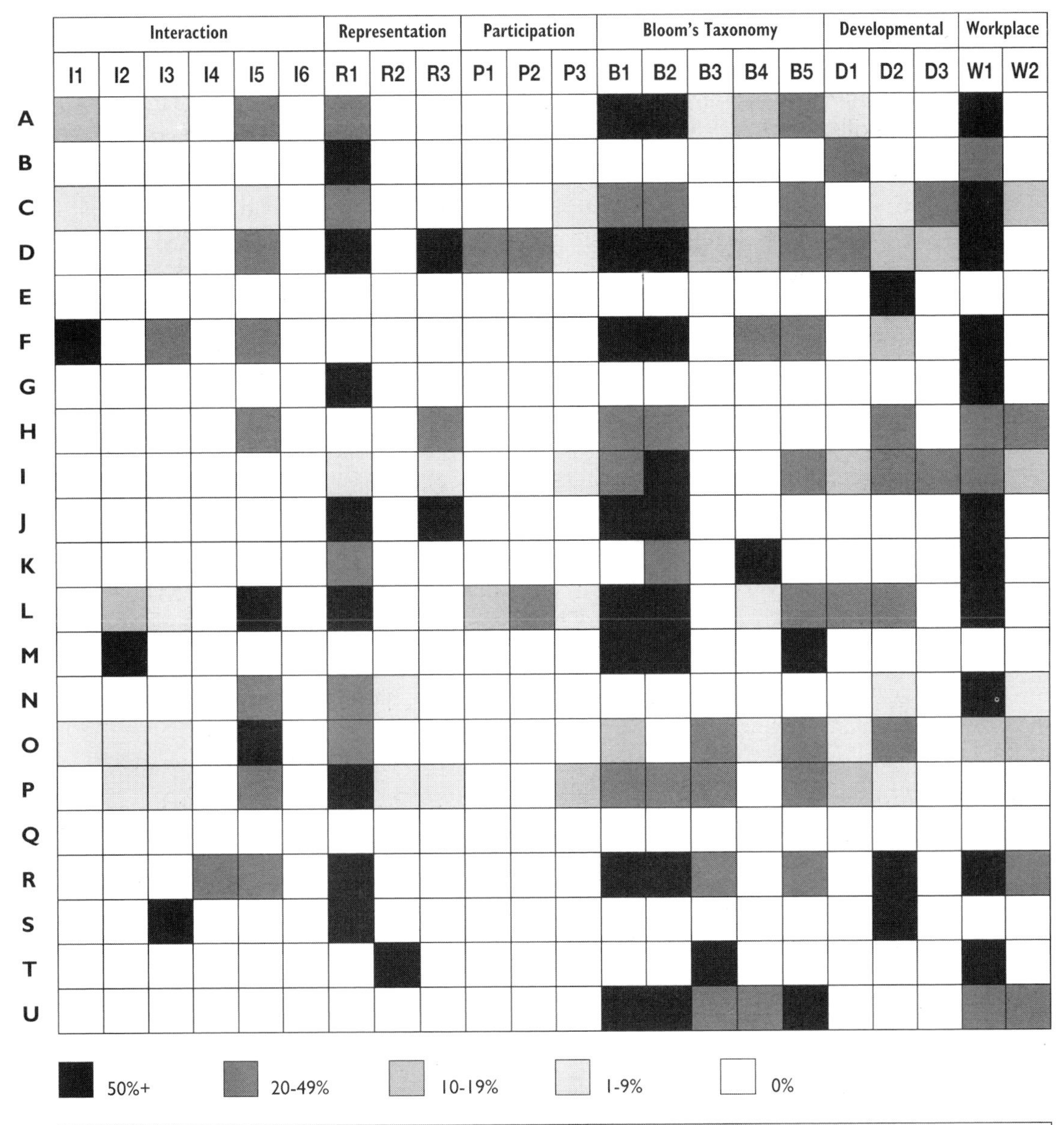

Interaction [I1–I6]

- 1 Multiple choice; 2 Open book; 3 IT-based; 4 Interactive; 5 Group element; 6 Role-play

Representation [R1–R3]

- 1 Oral; 2 Numeric; 3 Diagram/Pictorial

Participation [P1–P3]

- 1 Self-assess; 2 Peer assess; 3 Self-set element

Bloom's Taxonomy [B1–B5]

1 Analytic; 2 Evaluative; 3 Skills focus; 4 Primary research; 5 Theory focus

Developmental [D1–D3]

- 1 Reflective; 2 Process/Periodic; 3 Portfolio

Workplace [W1–W2]

- 1 Practice focus; 2 Case study

Figure 1 Overview of assessment tasks used by particular departments (A-U) at Level M

4. Tasks that could be mapped on to *Bloom's Taxonomy* (Bloom, 1956) and thus assess the higher order cognitive skills.
5. Tasks that included a *developmental* element and allowed for a deep approach to learning.
6. Tasks that simulated the *workplace*, so calling for the learner to marry theory with practice.

We finished with a taxonomy of 22 features, separated into six main strands.

Results

Figure 1 shows the general results of the Master's courses we studied as part of our research. The departments studied are shown on the vertical axis and the six strands on the horizontal axis. The table underneath the figure describes each of the 22 features we identified.

The darker filled cells in the diagram indicate more use of a particular feature than the lighter ones. For example, department J appears to have a strong commitment to oral and diagrammatic assessment, to testing analytic and evaluative skills and to using tasks that focus on practice. In contrast, department P uses a much wider range of assessment types, without relying on any one in particular. Looking down rather than across the diagram, it can be seen that some features (e.g., W1, practice-focus) are used widely across the institution, many (e.g., I5, B4, D2) are used with varying frequency, and some (e.g., R2, P3) are hardly used at all.

Discussion

It was clear, therefore, from the data that a wide range of assessment tasks were used in the institution and that departments used these tasks in very different ways. The problem that faced us as we started to design our pre-Master's programme was how best to prepare prospective students to enter these departments and study successfully.

Our first thoughts were that we should not have any stand-alone EAP or research skills classes, but that we should integrate EAP and research skills into the subject classes that our students were doing as part of their pre-Master's programme. This would mean that any assessment types that the students needed to be familiar with would arise naturally out of these subject classes.

A pre-Master's programme was therefore suggested to consist of a one-semester (12 teaching weeks) programme made up of two specialist subject modules and a research project module. The purpose of the specialist subject modules was to teach the subject along with the associated language, communication and study skills. The two subject modules would have English as an integral part of the subject modules, and the research project module would consist of three equal components: subject content; language and skills; research methods and study skills. However, on further investigation we realized that this was likely to be very costly, create a number of small classes and be difficult to administer.

Table 1 shows the programme that we then developed, using the research methods and project module as the vehicle for developing language and communication skills, rather than the specialist subject modules. We knew it to be the case that different disciplines favoured different genres (Becher, 1989; Gillett, Hammond & Martala, 2009). A balance needed to be struck between generic and subject-specific assessment and this was achieved in the design of the research project module, which fused English and research skills. As we knew that the programme would be preparing students for three broad subject areas: engineering and physical sciences; life sciences and computer science, we decided to base the module on the research skills needed for the scientific method of observation, hypothesis and experimentation. We tracked the assessment types used in the subject-specific modules and incorporated the tasks into our course outline – for example, writing a scientific abstract.

Table 1 International pre-Master's: Programme outline

	Specialist subject 1 15 credits	**Specialist subject 2 15 credits**	**Research methods 15 credits**	**English 15 credits**
Subject teaching input	Lecture + seminar/workshop	Lecture + seminar/workshop	Lectures, workshops + subject supervision	English in academic contexts
English language and skills input	Subject-specific language & skills	Subject-specific language & skills	Research –related language & skills	General language skills

Our earlier research and knowledge of the literature had made us acutely conscious of the importance of building variety and flexibility into our assessment tasks (QAA, 2006). We knew that we needed to design a course that followed the four areas outlined by Dearing (1997), namely, the development of knowledge and understanding; cognitive/intellectual skills; key/transferable skills and practical skills. We also knew that in order to prepare students for assessment at Master's level we needed to create tasks that promoted autonomy in the learner, provided the opportunity to handle complex and competing knowledge and to develop an awareness of professional practice.

In order to achieve this aim, we selected from our 22 features those that most closely matched these hallmarks of good practice and built them into our assessment strategy, using them either for summative or formative assessment. The features we selected are taken from each of the six strands, ensuring a fair representation across the taxonomy. They were, in turn:

Interaction: Group element (used for formative tasks); *Representation*: Oral; *Participation*: Self-assess; *Bloom's Taxonomy*: Analytic; Evaluative; Skills focus; Primary research; Theory focus; *Developmental*: Reflective; Process/Periodic; and *Workplace*: Practice focus.

We developed four assessment tasks for the research module and mapped the selected features to them closely.

Research proposal. A pro-forma is supplied for students to complete. It is designed to orient the students towards their future research. As such, it calls upon the student to identify an area of research (B1 – Analytic), consider some key theories (B5 – Theory focus), and outlines a provisional time frame for their research (D2 – Process/Periodic). In doing so, it also anticipates a task that the student may meet in the workplace, so preparing them professionally (W1 – Practice focus).

Reflective diary. This is another pro-forma that the student completes on a weekly basis (D2 – Process/Periodic). They reflect upon their progress to date (D1 – Reflective), consider any difficulties they have experienced and determine how to resolve them (P1 – Self-assess). They continuously match their abilities to the requirements of the research task (B2 – Evaluative).

Research project. This is the main assignment for the module. The component parts require the student to bring together relevant literature, primary research and application of theory to practice (B1-B2 – Analytic, Evaluative; B4-B5 – Primary research, Theory focus). Once again, the assignment orients the student towards their professional career (W1 – Practice focus).

Oral presentation. The final assignment requires the student to report their findings orally (R1 – Oral). They have to select the salient parts of their research and construct a coherent narrative for their audience (B1-B2 – Analytic, Evaluative).

Of the remaining features on our taxonomy, we felt confident that they would be addressed in sufficient detail in the subject-specific modules that made up the remainder of the programme, and each of the subjects would have English language integrated into them. We also knew that the research methods module was bolstered by the English Language component of the programme, as this had been designed to follow closely the various elements of researching and writing a project and to deliver the requisite language skills at each step. More generic elements of academic writing would be covered in the English strand.

Conclusion

Our earlier research (Gillett & Hammond, 2009) provided details of the wide range of assessment types required of students at Master's level. We then used it to analyze the kind of assessment tasks in a range of subjects studied by pre-Master's students at our institution. We knew that we had to design a programme which had an assessment regime that was developmental, relevant and fair, and wanted to capitalize on the experience we had gained from previous practice. We have set out to demonstrate that a careful mapping of discrete features of assessment to specific tasks can result in a product of relevance and value to learners across a spectrum of disciplines, and one that prepares them properly for study and research at Master's level.

It is too soon to judge the success of this approach for our programme, although we are encouraged by preliminary results and feedback from students. We know from experience that preparatory programmes are invaluable in helping students to understand and adapt to a new academic culture, acting as a place of safety where they can experiment and learn from mistakes. To be effective, assessment in such programmes has to anticipate the type of activities students will meet in the next stage; even to look beyond there to professional behaviours. This means that assessment has to be personalized as far as possible and tailored to specific disciplines, rather than staying at a generic level where one size has to fit all. It also has to provide tasks that develop the learner's capacity for reflection and monitoring of their own progress. This then calls for an approach where assessment is carefully staged, developed in sequence and, over time, is providing adequate formative assessment alongside the summative and engaging the learner more fully in these processes.

REFERENCES

Becher, T. (1989). *Academic tribes and territories.* Buckingham: The Society for Research into Higher Education and Open University Press.

Biggs, J. (2003). *Teaching for quality learning at university* (2nd edn.). Buckingham: Open University Press.

Bloom, B. S. (ed.) (1956). *Taxonomy of educational objectives: The classification of educational goals.* New York: David McKay.

Brown, S. (2004). Assessment for learning. *Learning and Teaching in Higher Education, 1,* 81–89.

Dearing, R. (1997). *Higher education in the learning society.* Norwich: National Committee of Inquiry into Higher Education.

Habeshaw, S., Gibbs, G. & Habeshaw, T. (1993). *53 interesting ways to assess your students.* Bristol: Technical and Educational Services.

Gillett, A. J. & Hammond, A. C. (2009). Mapping the maze of assessment: An investigation into practice. *Active Learning in Higher Education, 10,* 120–137. doi: 10.1177/1469787409104786.

Gillett, A. J., Hammond, A. C. & Martala, M. (2009). *Successful academic writing.* London: Pearson Education.

Knight, P. (2002). Summative assessment in higher education: Practices in disarray. *Studies in Higher Education, 27,* 275–286.

Moon, J. (2002). *The module & programme development handbook: A practical guide to linking.* London: Kogan Page.

Quality Assurance Agency (2006). *Code of practice for the assurance of academic quality and standards in higher education. Section 6: Assessment of students.* Retrieved May 31, 2007 from: http://www.qaa.ac.uk/academicinfrastructure/codeofpractice/

Rowntree, D. (1987). *Assessing students: How shall we know them*? (2nd edn.) London: Kogan Page.

Rust, C. (2002). The impact of assessment on student learning: How can the research literature practically help to inform the development of departmental assessment strategies and learner-centred assessment practices? *Active Learning in Higher Education, 3,* 145–158.

Sadler, D. R. (1998). Formative assessment: Revisiting the territory. *Assessment in Education: Principles, Policy and Practice, 5,* 77–84.

SECTION IV

Specificity and assessment

Bruce Howell

Preparation for English-medium study = academic English test preparation?

Introduction

Increasing numbers of students applying to study at English language-medium universities worldwide has led to a huge demand for formal certification of academic English language proficiency. In the UK, the number of non-EU students studying in the UK doubled between the mid-1990s and the mid-2000s (Universities UK, 2009). Although the UK's attraction for 'globally mobile' students is decreasing in relative worldwide terms, annual arrivals continue to rise – from about 200,000 in 2003 to more than 250,000 in 2008 (British Council et al., 2004; HESA, 2010). The vast majority of these students will take an EAP test on at least one occasion. Because such tests influence students' futures, test preparation demand grows alongside test demand. While demand for 'training for a test' is an expected phenomenon, there is a danger of the short-term goal of achieving the test grade required for unconditional acceptance becoming all-encompassing at the expense of developing knowledge and skills that will be most useful at university.

As a case study, perceived needs for preparation for the Test of English for Educational Purposes (TEEP) will be discussed. Experiments in creating and using test-related familiarization and preparation materials are evaluated here, reaching the conclusion that while direct preparation of some sort for an EAP test is unavoidable, it is not necessarily beneficial to scores, but will be beneficial to students if contextualised within a broader EAP framework.

What is this test and how do I prepare for it?'

'Preparation', in the context of getting ready to study abroad, means reaching readiness for coping with future study expectations, cultural differences and language demands; but when having to reach a certain grade on an EAP test represents the last hurdle to clear, 'preparation' can come to mean simply achieving the required grade in a test, and not looking beyond.

An important distinction assessment specialists make is *achievement testing*, that is, testing what has been taught, and *proficiency testing*. Definitions given by Richards et al. (1992) are:

- achievement tests – 'with reference to a particular course of study'
- proficiency tests – 'not linked to a particular course of instruction'

A proficiency test by definition measures a generic ability level, and supposedly therefore is not something that is designed to be 'prepared for' or 'revised'. Nevertheless, a common way to deal with preparation is practice, practice, practice – in other words, attempting a large number of actual or simulated test tasks – a method often encouraged by teachers.

In certain types of proficiency testing, standards may be limited and easy to set, so a restricted syllabus can easily be created, and to some extent focus on practising the actual test 'event' is appropriate. To use the British Cycling Proficiency Test or the series of piano grades assessed by ABRSM (2009) as examples, standards are relatively easy to define, well established and not the source of extensive debate. In the case of the piano, not all aspects of playing the instrument are covered – for instance improvisational skills – but there is little argument to expand the piano grades' remit, since qualifications are generally not required for genres such as jazz. Set courses of study, which on the whole mean repeatedly practising the relevant pieces until they are perfected, can therefore be set. Language, on the other hand, is a skill so diverse that it is almost impossible to reach a consensus on what defines standards. It is very difficult to define various proficiency levels without going into enormous amounts of detail, as can be seen from the ongoing work on the Common European Framework of Reference (CEFR). So how should candidates prepare for an EAP proficiency test? Pure 'practice' using past papers is inappropriate, but no preparation at all is unsatisfactory, so a middle-way is required.

Two different needs

The diagram below represents two types of need of a student whose first language is not English coming to study in the UK: the left-hand one being obvious and the right-hand one being an official necessity. There is overlap, the extent of which will depend on many factors – the two needs would coincide if the assessment taken pre-arrival truly represented accurate measures of all skills necessary to function successfully as a student in the UK.

I need the skills necessary to be able to function successfully as a student in the UK

I need to get a ... [insert required grade here]

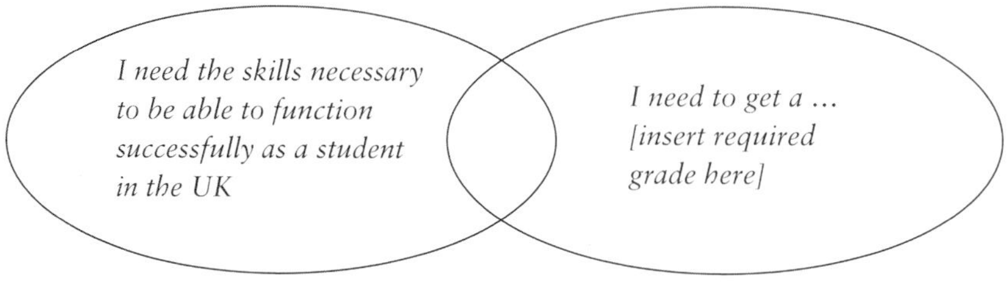

The separation shown here is one of energy focus: too much focus on the right-hand mindset may act to the detriment of the other. The main reason that the two needs do not usually coincide is practical. Debate is ongoing as to what should be assessed in order to determine overall EAP levels, but few would argue that *all* relevant EAP skills can be covered within a single assessment lasting somewhere between two and four hours. The way in which and the extent to which skills and knowledge can practically be assessed means that EAP tests *approximate* levels, but cannot provide *comprehensive* information about preparedness for language use at UK universities. Despite recent improvements, tests, by their nature, can only sample the full array of desired skills and sub-skills (e.g., Alderson, 2009:628). Below is a sample of desired language-related study skills that a short test simply cannot measure to any great extent, no matter how valid and reliable it may be.

Ability to:

- research, through reading extensively
- incorporate information/ideas from various sources into an essay or presentation
- respond to lecturer/teacher/tutor feedback
- manage a heavy workload over a number of weeks

What is 'preparation'?

Having accepted that preparation of some sort is needed specifically for tests, let us approach test preparation by firstly *familiarization* to avoid shock, confusion or stress, and secondly *strategies for achieving a higher score*. Testing organizations should freely provide information for candidates which help with familiarization, such as:

- format – what the test looks like, number of papers, time allowed, number and type of questions, type of answers expected
- explanations of test design
- practical details – where and when the test will be, regulations, e.g., what (not) to bring
- experience ('mock' practice)

Candidates demand strategies for achieving a high enough score, and improving relevant language skills should be considered as the best way to do this. However, the high-stakes nature of EAP assessment means that the following may also be given attention:

- memorization techniques
- ways of guessing effectively
- ways of 'fooling' examiners
- cheating methods such as identity swapping

This list clearly features undesirable tactics, and if a school or publisher were to encourage such activities this would be deemed unethical (Hamp-Lyons, 1998). While preventing cheating is beyond the control of the test writers, the design of item types plays a major role in allowing for, or even encouraging, some of the above tactics.

A case in point: the TEEP

The pre-sessional assessment system at the University of Reading has previously been explained at BALEAP events (Howell & Slaght, 2007 & 2009). This system combines use of TEEP as a standardized measure, alongside a series of continuous assessment tests and observations, in an attempt to make the final assessment comprehensive, covering the four main skills, observable sub-skills such as pronunciation, *and* extensive study skills such as those listed above. Students receive oral and written explanations and assurances that TEEP skills are a sub-set of those covered on the course, alongside a limited amount of 'mock' practice so as to make them content with relatively little direct 'TEEP preparation'. Although the indirect preparation approach sometimes takes a number of weeks to be fully understood, it is successful on the whole and has become a vital part of the course. The original approach of treating the test as an 'independent' measure resulted in endless questions from students, indicating test anxiety in the absence of information.

However, growth of the TEEP has resulted in catering for an additional audience: those not yet in the UK or on pre-sessional courses. Without the background that pre-sessional students receive, candidates for the stand-alone TEEP bring demands of the 'how do I prepare?' type. This demand came from students who at best were able to attend short and part-time courses, so the decision was made that the TEEP writers/markers/administrators themselves would create teaching materials for non-pre-sessional students which could be condensed into approximately 30 hours.

From the outset, the aim was to produce materials which, in order of importance:

- support candidates in achieving higher grades through improvement of relevant language skills
- contextualize and expand on what is expected at a UK university
- relate TEEP skills to the wider concept of EAP
- give familiarization through experience (mock tests)
- give familiarization through exam tips

In other words, materials are a condensed (not comprehensive) EAP course with additional familiarization and practice of the test format. The exam tips, such as giving advice on transferring answers to answer sheets, are designed so that candidates can avoid pitfalls – 'trick' tactics are avoided! Teacher's notes had to be very detailed, providing guidance and further context for teachers who may not have experience of EAP or UK universities.

The first trials of these materials in preparation courses took place in Taiwan from late 2007 to early 2009, designed to complement the TEEP test administrations, which took place on completion of the course. A relatively small minority (about 100 in total) of those who took the tests also took the course, for a small fee. The students were exclusively Taiwanese, and predominantly in their early 20s.

The outcome of these trials was that both students and teachers were generally happy with the quality of the materials and the contextualization they gave, so that a much clearer picture was created of what to expect in the exam. Additionally, such materials saved a lot of time for teachers, who would otherwise have had to investigate for themselves the aims and content of TEEP, and work out a teaching approach. Teachers filled out feedback forms as they used the materials, which helped develop the course. A reoccurring request was for 'more practice', reflecting perhaps that the balance between quantities of test-like activities and contextualization has not yet been perfected.

Table 1 Estimated proficiency gain – all available data

	Mean grade BEFORE (IELTS, TEEP, TOEFL equivalents*)	Mean grade AFTER (TEEP)	Difference
no course (n=121)	5.33	5.66	+0.33
attended course (n=33)	5.39	5.59	+0.20
all (n=154)	5.34	5.64	+0.30

** TEEP and IELTS use a similar 0-9 scale which was assumed to be equivalent for the purposes of this study. TOEFL iBT/TEEP equivalences are based on the University of Reading's own estimate.*

An informal study: is test preparation effective?

From the approximately 600 candidates who took TEEP in Taiwan during 2007–2009, 154 records were found of measured proficiency levels before TEEP preparation courses began (BEFORE on the below tables), and 33 of these students completed courses. BEFORE grades were mostly from a recent IELTS test, with some TOEFL or previous TEEP grades. These data were gathered in retrospect to carry out a mini-comparison of BEFORE grades and those achieved after the courses (shown as AFTER). Table 1 shows estimated proficiency gain by those taking the course, compared to those who did not.

When we compare 'no course' and 'attended course' groups, the figures disappointingly show that the gain was apparently greater for candidates who did not attend the course! However, firm conclusions from these figures cannot really be made, for a number of reasons:

- lack of certainty about accuracy of BEFORE levels (received second-hand from local administrators)
- variability in time gap between the pre- and post-course grades (some BEFORE grades may have dated from more than a month before the course started)
- course variation from location to location in terms of class size, time of day and number of contact hours, and time over which the course was spread
- lack of information about the 'non-course' group – e.g., they would likely have been preparing in other ways
- assumed equivalence between IELTS, TEEP and TOEFL levels
- the relatively small numbers of students involved

The most probable explanation is that a 0–9 scale which measures 'nil' to 'total' ability is not sensitive enough to make meaningful comparisons of expected gain after only 30 hours' study. Time needed for proficiency gain is difficult to determine, and according to de Jong (2009) is usually underestimated, since it tends to increase with level. Other researchers have reported that score gain depends to a large extent on initial proficiency level (e.g., Read & Hayes, 2003), and it does seem that some students plateau at TEEP levels 5.0, 5.5 or 6.0. TEEP's Standard Error of Measurement

(SEM) of ±0.3 (unpublished University of Reading data 2004–2009) also means the small differences shown above should be treated with caution.

Another explanation is that preparation courses are simply not effective in terms of increasing scores. Research has been mixed in this area. A recent article (Butler, 2009) highlighted that shorter and intensive courses tend to be less effective than longer and more gradual ones. Both Nguyen (2007) and Coomber (1998) found it difficult to generalize about test preparation effect, since there is such variation between types of test, approaches to preparation, and how improvement is measured. In order for any real conclusion to be drawn from the TEEP teaching materials, a much more involved study would be needed, comparing length and intensiveness of courses, and approach taken by teachers.

What does it all mean?

Whether preparation is effective in the sense of increasing grades seems uncertain, since so many factors are involved, and anyway gains are difficult to measure accurately. Researchers into IELTS have also noted that individual skills may develop at different rates (Elder & O'Loughlin, 2003).

Bialy (2003) concluded that a communicative approach towards preparing for a communicative test was more effective that rote memorization. Roberts (2002) concluded that test preparation can be detrimental to language progression, if approached in the wrong way. Roberts also found that both students and teachers like preparation materials, but perhaps for different reasons, and Green (2006) indicates that it may be teachers or materials – not students – who are to blame for unprincipled test preparation practices. Course designers for EAP test preparation do seem to have a heavy weight on their shoulders.

Although this mini-study merely adds to the inconclusiveness of the value of preparation, anecdotal evidence convinces me that the principled approach to preparation the TEEP writers have taken works to the benefit of all stakeholders. TEEP preparation courses aim to aid *understanding* of UK study, by contextualizing activities, explaining *why* they are being undertaken and how they relate to the 'real' student experience. It is hoped that by guiding students through tasks and showing the various ways of tackling them, while de-emphasising the need to always be 'right' or 'perfect', instils *confidence*, too. This building of understanding and confidence is done through commentary in the students' pages which is explicated in more detail in the teachers' pages, and has been welcomed by users. Indeed, it is somewhat ironic that, when the materials were trialled with pre-sessional teachers and students at the University of Reading, there were calls to incorporate them permanently into pre-sessional courses. It is hoped that this desire comes from the benefits to language and study-skill development the materials provide, as well as – rather than simply – the belief that grades will be improved.

References

Alderson, J. C. (2009). Test review: Test of English as a Foreign Language™: Internet-based Test. *Language Testing, 26/4*, 621–631.

Associated Board of the Royal Schools of Music (ABRSM) (2009). *Piano Syllabus booklets.* Retrieved November 2009 from http://www.abrsm.org/?page=exams/gradedMusicExams/latestSyllabuses.html#Piano

Bialy, J. (2003). *IELTS Speaking Test preparation in the People's Republic of China: Communicative approaches and rote-memorization compared.* MA dissertation, University of Surrey.

British Council, Universities UK and IDP (2004). *Vision 2020: Forecasting International Student Mobility, A UK Perspective.* Retrieved November 2009 from http://www.britishcouncil.org/eumd_-_vision_2020.pdf

Butler, M. (2009). Less is More? *EL Gazette*, October 2009.

Coomber, J. (1998). *Are Test Preparation Programs Really Effective? Evaluating an IELTS Preparation Course.* MA dissertation, University of Surrey.

Elder, C. & O'Loughlin, K. (2003). Investigating the relationship between intensive EAP training and band score gains on IELTS. *IELTS Research Reports, 4*, IELTS Australia. Retrieved November 2009 from http://www.ielts.org/researchers/research/volumes/volume_4.aspx

Green, A. (2006). Washback to the learner: Learner and teacher perspectives on IELTS preparation course expectations and outcomes. *Assessing Writing, 11/2*, 113–134.

Hamp-Lyons, L. (1998). Ethical test preparation practice: the case of TOEFL. *TESOL Quarterly, 32/2*, 329–337.

Higher Education Statistics Agency (HESA) (2010). *Statistics: Student Data (Table 1).* Retrieved July 2010 from http://www.hesa.ac.uk/dox/pressOffice/sfr142/SFR142_Table1.pdf

Howell, B. & Slaght, J. (2007). TEEP: A Course-Driven Assessment Measure. In O. Alexander (Ed.), *Proceedings of the 2005 joint BALEAP/SATEFL conference: New Approaches to Materials Development for Language Learning* (pp.253–263), Bern: Peter Lang.

Howell, B. & Slaght, J. (2009). Action Research into Pre-sessional Students' Differentiation of Assessments: Using Findings to Improve Courses. In O. Alexander (Ed.), *Proceedings of the 2007 BALEAP conference: English in a globalizing world: English as an academic lingua franca* (pp.87–94). Bern: Peter Lang.

de Jong, J. H. A. L. (2009). *Unwarranted claims about CEF alignment of some international English language tests.* Presentation at The 6th Annual conference of the European Association for Language Testing and Assessment, June 2009, Turku, Finland.

Nguyen, T. N. H. (2007). Effects of test preparation on test performance – the case of the IELTS and TOEFL iBT Listening tests. *Melbourne Papers in Language Testing, 12*, 1–24.

Read, J. & Hayes, B. (2003). The impact of IELTS on preparation for academic study in New Zealand. *IELTS Research Reports Volume 4*, IELTS Australia. Retrieved November 2009 from http://www.ielts.org/researchers/research/volumes/volume_4.aspx

Richards, J. C., Platt, J. & Platt, H. (1992). *Dictionary of Language Teaching and Applied Linguistics.* Harlow: Longman.

Roberts, M. (2002). TOEFL preparation: what are our Korean students doing and why?' *Korea TESOL Journal, 5*, 81–106.

Universities UK (2009). *Higher Education in Facts and Figures.* Retrieved November 2009 from http://www.universitiesuk.ac.uk/NEWSROOM/FACTS-AND-FIGURES/Pages/Higher-Education-in-Facts-and-Figures.aspx

Dorothy Adams-Metaxopoulou and Phil Morris

Towards guided learning: assessing the impact of Language Learning Advisory Services

Introduction

This article will present the findings of a pilot study into the effectiveness of the Language Learning Advisory Service (LLAS) at a large metropolitan university, and will discuss opportunities for further research into this service; as will be explained, conclusions drawn from the achievements and limitations of this pilot study have formed the basis of a much larger research project. The article will begin by providing a background to the study, discussing research into the areas of test anxiety and Language Learning Advisors, and will then give a brief overview of the provision that the LLAS at Manchester Metropolitan University (MMU) offers to our international students. Finally, the study itself, its methodology, findings and conclusions will be discussed.

Background

The research for this present paper forms part of a larger project within MMU to meet the needs of a growing population of international students who come to our university to study. To provide just one example of research in this area, Li's (2007) study of Chinese-speaking research students studying in the UK points to a need for universities in English-speaking countries to offer adequate and appropriate provision for the general well-being of their international students, as well as for their language skills and subject-specific education. The Chinese students in the study described feeling alienated, and the conclusion drawn is that this may lead to de-motivation and anxiety. Of particular interest to this present study is the way in which the LLAS, which will be discussed in the next section, can be shown to have a positive effect on the learning experience of international students, especially from the point of view of test anxiety. It is our contention that, if we can in some way reduce such anxiety, we can increase the performance levels that these students may attain.

Eysenck's (1979) study suggests that low levels of anxiety may indeed increase performance in tests; so-called 'facilitative anxiety' leads to increased motivation with attendant benefits for the learner. However, the negative relationship between anxiety and achievement or performance seems to have been confirmed: in reading, Saito, Garza & Horwitz (1999); in writing, Cheng, Horwitz & Schallert (1999); in speaking, Liu (2006); and in listening, Mills, Pajares & Herron (2006); Elkhafaifi (2005). In other words, there seems to be considerable evidence that anxiety directly and negatively affects test scores among second language learners (Horwitz, 1986; MacIntyre & Gardner, 1991b). Indeed, MacIntyre & Gardner (1991a:103) state that, 'in some cases, anxiety produces some of the highest simple correlations of attitudes with achievement'.

Our study focused specifically on test anxiety; our study group were IELTS candidates, amongst whom a certain amount of test anxiety is to be expected, given the potential impact on their future of a low score in the IELTS test. Our aim was to establish whether the recently-founded LLAS could be shown to assist to some degree in lowering test anxiety levels.

The Language Learning Advisory Service

The LLAS at MMU is based in the recently refurbished, state-of-the-art Media Centre of the Department of Languages. Despite considerable student interest in the new facilities, and to cite the findings of the Critical Interventions for Enhanced Learning Project in 2000, it was obvious that simply having a Media Centre was no guarantee that students would access the facilities and no guarantee that those who used the facilities would do so to maximum effect. The essential aim of the service is to advise students on how to become autonomous learners; in other words, to use resources and time more effectively, to access and use a range of appropriate strategies to support their language learning in the main four skills and to show a more independent approach. This particular study focused on test preparation in order to discover whether the service could in some way be shown to assist students in lowering their test anxiety levels in preparation for the all-important IELTS test.

The service is supervised by two EAP lecturers, who coordinate the work of six fully-trained student ambassadors as part of the university's commitment to enhancing student employability.

A typical Language Learning Advisory session

At the outset it needs to be stated that there is no typical session. The service mainly operates on a drop-in basis, which means that it is largely unknown who will attend, and for what reason. Although all advisors work to a specific framework, the sessions are highly personalized and focus on the individual student's needs, lacks and wants. However, the starter session usually lasts for 30 minutes and tends to be structured in the following way:

- Establishing a rapport and explaining the role of the Language Learning Advisor. This involves explaining the purpose of the LLAS and making

clear that it does not offer private language tuition.
- Needs analysis.
- Creating an individualized study plan.
- Suggestions/recommendations for self-directed learning. Once these have been made, the advisor's role is to take the student through the resources and ensure that s/he will be able to use them independently.

This would normally conclude the starter session; the advisor then suggests that the student calls back at a later date to discuss their progress and/or receive further advice and recommendations. It is also made clear that if any of the materials suggested prove to be inappropriate for any reason, such as level of difficulty, this should be discussed at the next suitable drop-in session. Once these suggestions have been made, the responsibility for any further contact with the LLAS remains with the learner.

As indicated above, the LLAS does not offer language instruction *per se*; rather, it provides materials and skills-training which can assist the student in the process of developing self-directed learning, because 'the focus is not on product [...], but on the processes of learning to learn, learning to be autonomous' (Mozzon-MacPherson, 2007). Consequently, members of staff are trained not only to give advice on a wide range of materials and learning strategies, but also to address issues such as learner motivation and anxiety. Of particular interest to this present study, then, was whether the LLAS could be shown to have a positive effect on the learning experience, especially from the point of view of test anxiety. Clearly, any attempt to assess the impact of a service which promotes autonomous learning is particularly problematic; indeed as Reinders & Lazaro (2008) point out, learning gains in this area cannot easily be attributed. It is difficult to know, or to show, whether learning has taken place as a result of actions taken on the advice given and, if so, to what extent this may be the case. In this study, therefore, we have taken both a quantitative and qualitative approach in order to better assess any possible gains.

The subjects

The group chosen for the pilot study comprised 90 international students who were enrolled on a 30-week course to prepare for the IELTS examination in June, 2009, in order to enter the university – in most cases at postgraduate level – in the following academic year. The subjects were principally, but not exclusively, from Middle Eastern countries, French-speaking African countries, China and Taiwan and primarily, though not exclusively, in the age-range of 19–25 (86%). In order to enrol on this course, the students had provided evidence of a minimum qualification of IELTS 4.0, or a TOEFL score of 450 or above. Participation in this research was optional, and 27 students elected to take part. The control group was therefore considered to be the remaining 63 students who had chosen not to make use of the LLAS. One student from the control group returned home before the research was completed, and the corresponding data was removed from the study.

Research methods

In October, 2008, all 90 students were given a questionnaire to assess their levels of anxiety about listening tests, and were then given an IELTS-style listening test. The questionnaire was based on Horwitz et al.'s (1986) Foreign Language Classroom Anxiety Scale, a 33-point questionnaire which relates to three general sources of anxiety: communication apprehension, tests and fear of negative evaluation. The questionnaire for this present study was limited to only ten questions, selected and adapted from Horwitz et al. (1986), and from Elkhafaifi (2005), to directly relate to listening test anxiety. A five-point Likert scale was used, with answers ranging from *strongly agree* to *strongly disagree*. Example questions are:

> Question 2: 'I get nervous when the listening passage is read only once during a listening test.'
> Question 3: 'I am nervous when I am listening to English if I am not familiar with the topic.'

And the key question for this research:

> Question 7: 'I am very nervous before a listening test.'

The 27 students who had chosen to take an active part in the research were asked to register with the LLAS. Each student had one 30-minute session with an advisor, and was offered subsequent 30-minute sessions throughout the study, typically at the rate of one session per week, until the course had ended. At the end of March, 2009, the 89 remaining students were given an identical questionnaire to assess their listening test anxiety levels. A second IELTS-style listening test was then administered and the results were analyzed. In addition, qualitative data taken from participants who attended the LLAS throughout the study were also analyzed.

Research questions

The primary questions that we sought to answer with this study are the following:

1. To what extent can any reduction in test anxiety be demonstrated among students who have used the LLAS?
2. Is there any noticeable improvement in listening test scores among students who have used the LLAS?
3. Can any correlation be shown between the two sets of findings?

Results

As can be seen from the results in Figure 1, the responses to the second test anxiety questionnaire seemed to reveal a greater shift towards a reduction in anxiety among the group that had availed itself of the LLAS, when compared to the result for the group that had not (the control group); we provide the data for what we consider to be the key question, Question 7 (see above). Similarly, Figure 2 seems to indicate an increase in the listening scores, from October, 2008, to March, 2009, for those who had attended the LLAS in the interim: 78.6% of the subjects in the study group showed a marked improvement in the second listening test, compared to 71% of the subjects in the control group.

These results seem to indicate, then, that those students who had chosen to attend the service experienced a decrease in listening test anxiety levels over the six-month period of the study, while also showing an improvement in their listening test scores. The results for the control group also show a general decrease in anxiety, accompanied by a general improvement in test scores, and this is to be expected from a group of students who have lived and studied in the UK for six months; the figures for this group are not, however, quite as significant as they are for the study group.

Study Group	**October 2008**	**March 2009**
Strongly agree	22%	6%
Agree	41%	28%
Neither agree nor disagree	15%	39%
Disagree	15%	23%
Strongly disagree	7%	5%

Control Group	**October 2008**	**March 2009**
Strongly agree	19%	11%
Agree	38%	32%
Neither agree nor disagree	15%	19%
Disagree	18%	28%
Strongly disagree	10%	10%

Figure 1 Listening test anxiety scores to Question 7 for October, 2008, and March, 2009, by group

Listening test results for the 27 students who attended the LLAS (study group)	
increase in score	78.6%
same score	7.1%
decrease in score	14.3%

Listening test results for the 62 students who did not attended the LLAS (control group)	
increase in score	71%
same score	0%
decrease in score	29%

Figure 2 Comparison of listening test scores for October, 2008, and March, 2009, by group

Discussion

Of course, as with much research into second language acquisition, it is difficult to pinpoint the exact reasons for this disparity between the two groups, which may indeed be due to a number of factors; more research is clearly required. It is important to remember that this was a voluntary exercise; logic and experience tell us that students who put themselves forward for such studies are often the more committed learners, and that such learners generally tend to show more rapid improvement. Even if this is the case, this does not reflect badly on the LLAS. The service provides extra opportunities for such students to practise language in a controlled setting and, more importantly, to receive advice on how to become more autonomous; the fact that it is difficult to provide irrefutable evidence to prove a correlation between this activity and reduced test anxiety levels does not prove that one does not exist. Indeed, one visit to the LLAS may well be all that certain learners require; as Fu (1999) points out, 'a seed may have been sown', even at the starter session. Clearly, any attempt to collect empirical evidence to prove such a claim is intrinsically problematic; for this reason, in addition to the quantitative data given above, we also provide a selection of qualitative data, gathered from student interviews during and immediately after the study:

> (1) 'The Language Learning Advisory Service is a great idea. My problem was that I can't use pronunciation as often as I want. I told this to an advisor and he give me pronunciation to do at home.'
>
> B., male, native Arabic speaker, 24

Extract 1

The advisor recommended that B. worked on the 'Tell Me More' voice recognition software program (which B. refers to as 'pronunciation') and indicated which sections of the program best addressed the issues facing B. in both production and reception. The student became highly motivated in his desire to further improve his pronunciation, as is evidenced by his request for materials to use at home.

> (2) 'I was very impressed with the Media Centre. The advisors are very good ... they make students feel comfortable.'
>
> K., male, native Chinese speaker, 26

Extract 2

K. was a painfully shy student, who had been feeling very 'ashamed' of his *perceived* lack of ability. After meeting with one of the advisors (herself a non-native speaker), he realized that native-speaker-like RP is not the only model of pronunciation. He was very pleasantly surprised that someone who 'had an accent' was working as a Language Learning Advisor, and his confidence began to grow. Although, as previously stated, the correlation between the LLAS and a reduction in test anxiety is difficult to establish, the subsequent and significant improvement in his overall performance in the IELTS test may not be entirely coincidental.

> (3) T. believed that using the self-directed study resources suggested to her by the LLAS had helped her in the IELTS listening test and had also led to a significant improvement in her spoken English: 'I think it also helps me

> to speak more clearly too. I noticed that English people didn't look so confused when I speak with them!'
>
> T., female, native Arabic speaker, 23

Extract 3

The comment by this student illustrates one of the main problems faced by many of our students: their confidence is undermined when they fail to communicate successfully with native speakers. The advisor on duty soon realized that, although T. did not have any problems with English phonemes, she had little or no awareness of connected speech patterns, such as assimilation, elision, linking and intrusion, and suggested appropriate materials for T. to address these issues in her own time. Once her awareness was raised, listening became a much less daunting task and T. clearly feels that this has had a positive impact on her oral/aural skills; the effect on her self-confidence is evident in her comments.

> (4) 'I think I did much better in the last listening test.'
>
> G., female, native Arabic speaker, 24

Extract 4

The student in Extract 4 is speaking about her performance on the second IELTS listening paper, taken at the end of this study. Earlier in the study, she had been given resources to practise listening, and also guidance on strategies to use in the listening test. Again, although it is impossible to draw a direct correlation between test anxiety, performance and the impact of the LLAS, the fact that G.'s score was markedly higher in the listening test at the end of the study, *and that G. believed that it would be*, would again suggest that there is support for the findings of our quantitative evidence.

CONCLUSION

The results given above seem to show that, even in this relatively short-term study, a greater percentage of those who attended the LLAS showed an improvement in their listening test scores compared to those who did not attend; over the same period, listening test anxiety levels also appear to have dropped and, again, the changes were more marked among the study group than in the control group, who did not use the service. As has been stated, there are clearly a number of other factors that may be at play, thus making it unwise to suggest that the two factors are *directly* linked; nevertheless, learners' comments seem to reflect a belief that such a link indeed exists. Further research is clearly required, and a larger-scale project is now underway with the aim of establishing a link between the LLAS, test anxiety and test performance in all four sections of the IELTS test.

References

Cheng, Y., Horwitz, E. & Schallert, D. (1999). Language anxiety: differentiating writing and speaking components. *Language Learning, 49/3*, 417–446.

Elkhafaifi, H. (2005). Listening comprehension and anxiety in the Arabic language classroom. *Modern Language Journal, 89/2/*, 206–220.

Eysenck, M.W. (1979). Anxiety, learning and memory: a reconceptualization. *Journal of Research in Personality, 13*, 363–385.

Fu, G. (1999). Guidelines for productive language counselling: tools for implementing autonomy. In S. Cotterall & D. Crabbe, (Eds.), *Learner Autonomy in Language Learning: Defining the Field and Effecting* Change (pp.107–111). Frankfurt-am-Main: Peter Lang.

Horwitz, E. K. (1986). Preliminary evidence for the reliability and validity of a Foreign Language Anxiety Scale. *TESOL Quarterly, 20*, 559–562.

Horwitz, E. K. (2001). Language anxiety and achievement. *Annual Review of Applied Linguistics, 21*, 112–126.

Horwitz, E. K., Horwitz, M. B. & Cope, J. (1986). Foreign language classroom anxiety. *Modern Language Journal, 70/2*, 125–132.

Li, Daguo (2007). Coping with linguistic challenges in UK Higher Education: the use of strategies by Chinese research students. *Language Learning, 45/2/*, 205–219.

Liu, M. (2006). Anxiety in Chinese EFL students at different proficiency levels. *System, 34*, 301–316.

MacIntyre, P. D., & Gardner, R. C. (1991a). Methods and results in the study of foreign language anxiety: a review of the literature. *Language Learning, 41/1/*, 85–117.

MacIntyre, P. D., & Gardner, R. C. (1991b). Language anxiety: its relationship to other anxieties and to processing in native and second languages. *Language Learning, 41/4*, 513–534.

MacIntyre, P. D., Baker, S. C., Clement, R. & Donovan, L. A. (2002). Sex and age effects on willingness to communicate, anxiety, perceived competence, and L2 motivation among junior high school French immersion students. *Language Learning, 52/3*, 537–564.

Mills, N., Pajares, F., & Herron, C. (2006). A re-evaluation of the role of anxiety: self-efficacy, anxiety, and their relation to reading and listening proficiency. *Foreign Language Annals, 39*, 276–295.

Mozzon-McPherson, M. (2007). Supporting independent learning environments: an analysis of structures and roles of language learning advisors. *System, 35/1*, 66–92.

Reinders, H. & Lazaro, N. (2008). The assessment of self-access language learning: practical challenges. *Language Learning Journal, 36/1*, 55–64.

Saito Y., Garza, Y. J., & Horwitz, E. K. (1999). Foreign language reading anxiety. *Modern Language Journal, 83*, 202–218.

Ann Smith and John Hall

Managing assessed group projects in a UK foundation programme

Introduction

The management of assessed group projects is integral to promoting the key skill of effective teamwork in the University of Nottingham's Foundation Certificate Programme for Business and Social Sciences. The programme was developed with input from the receiving schools and the overall aims are to develop academic literacy; especially thinking skills, language skills, study skills and effective group work.

The Foundation Programme provides young international students with 50% EAP to activate their language knowledge and help them to manage their studies independently and 50% introductory content modules. The two 30-credit EAP modules integrate students' language knowledge with global issues content. Thus the group projects begin in the EAP classes and then transfer to the introductory content modules, where students hone skills required for their future academic programmes. Our aim in this paper is to consider ways to manage assessed group projects more effectively in order to develop the key skill of effective teamwork and to avoid and deal with group conflicts.

Why group projects?

Assessed group projects are integral to promoting the key transferable and professional skills identified at undergraduate level. Summers and Volet (2008:368) note '... students' early experiences at university are particularly important for their development of the necessary skills and willingness to engage in group work with people of other cultures.' In surveys of education and employers, interpersonal skills such as working with others and teamwork are ranked as the first or second most important transferable skill (CDELL, 2002). In particular, the Nottingham University Business School (NUBS) frequently uses group projects in undergraduate programmes. The *BA (Hons)*

Table 1 BA (Hons) Management Studies

Professional/Practical Skills
• Self-awareness, openness and sensitivity to diversity in terms of people, cultures, business and management issues. • Effective performance within a team environment, including leadership, team building, influencing and project management skills. • The ability to conduct research into business and management issues, either individually or as part of a team, including a familiarity with a range of business data and research resources and appropriate methodologies.
Transferable/Key Skills
• Learning to learn and developing an appetite for reflective, adaptive and collaborative learning. • The interpersonal skills for effective listening, negotiating, persuasion and presentation.

Management Studies, shown in Table 1, illustrates this; the underlining shows references to interpersonal skills and group transferable skills.

In academic settings at the University of Nottingham, teamwork is popular in seminars, workshops, lab sessions and projects (Thondhlana & Gao, 2009). Leki (2001:40) points out 'A large and mainly optimistic body of research exists on the benefits of group work among peers', especially in co-operative learning. However, a group is not just a random number of individuals. Ehrman & Dörnyei (1998:251) identify a cohesive group as one where group members have a commitment or moral obligation to the group's success within a supportive environment. In group work, students need to listen actively, elicit and question others, negotiate, clarify and probe as well as justifying opinions and perspectives on the spot. This promotes fluency, appropriacy, motivation and helps to build confidence. Colbeck, Campbell & Bjorklund (2000:80) note that '... incorporating group projects in first- and second-year courses should increase the likelihood that students will develop the interpersonal communication and conflict management skills that will enable them to derive the greatest benefits ...'

Thondhlana & Gao (2009:29) found that academic projects 'required systematic investigation and a greater amount of effort than other activities' and that group projects are becoming more prevalent. They also noted a problem with international students working in groups and found that none of the schools consulted were training students to work in groups, although one school employed a trial group project to develop skills. Robinson et al. (2001:348–349) also found international students had difficulty participating effectively in seminars or class discussions because they lack confidence and the ability to speak spontaneously. Academic discussion is definitely more challenging and complex than social interaction as students have to recall relevant knowledge, formulate and organize ideas quickly in negotiation and speak spontaneously. Basturkmen (1999, 2002) shows academic discussion to be extended and more indirect and complex than previously thought. It goes beyond 'the initial elicitation, informational or directive moves as speakers frequently provide extra information, justification or support for a point and often follow up over several turns'. More recent broader interpretations of negotiation also include interpersonal interaction, turn taking and topic transitions (Zhengdong, Davidson & Hamp-Lyons, 2008). So when breakdowns occur students have to adjust and restructure their language spontaneously.

Although many project groups have functioned effectively, others have experienced disagreements which have ranged from time management disputes to miscommunication of concerns or personality conflicts. Frequently, an uncommitted student, a slacker, an avoider or a domineering leader/ruler causes conflict. At other times, complications have developed from a difference of ideas or opinions, personality clashes, lack of assertiveness, worries about marks, task allocation or concerns about the management of group presentation. Ehrman & Dörnyei (1998:128) identify values, goal ideas and opinions as common problems as well as 'incongruity of personal styles and needs', which, according to Flowerdew (1998), may relate to cultural communication styles. So students need assistance in resolving such issues.

A ROUTE TO RESOLUTION

Following discussions within the Foundation team, a three-pronged route to resolve the disagreements experienced within group work projects was developed. The first stage involved creating a fair and transparent policy for the management of group work projects and a resolution procedure that would be transparent for both tutors and students and similar to those used by the NUBS undergraduate programmes to which most students progress. This ensures unbiased assessment of the group projects, in which all students receive the same mark for the group component unless *evidence* to the contrary is provided.

The second stage entailed developing students' awareness of group dynamics and possible causes of disagreement. As the Oral Communication and Study (OCS) module (see Table 2) was already scaffolding group dynamics and communication, this was extended. In addition, two assessed EAP group projects in the module developed cross-cultural communication, project planning and time management. The third stage entailed transferring the skills developed in OCS to authentic group projects with presentations in three of the content modules (see Table 2).

Table 2 Foundation Programme modules

Semester 1	Semester 2
EAP Modules	
Written Communication and Study (30 credits)	
Oral Communication and Study (30 credits)	
Other Content Modules	
Introduction to Information Technology (15 credits)	Introduction to Analytical Thought (15 credits)
Business: Introduction to Business Economics (15 credits) **OR** Social Science: Media and Texts: Society (15 credits)	Business: Introduction to Business Methods (15 credits) **OR** Social Science: Media and Texts: Culture (15 credits)

In addition, group projects are carefully chosen and designed to include a variety of tasks that combine content with a range of interpersonal communication skills. The careful selection of groups is an essential step, so tutors collaborate to ensure that students are mixed according to level, gender and mother tongue to encourage cross-cultural communication and guarantee English language practice. While group project information is explained in class and group engagement is monitored weekly by the tutors, much of the group work is done outside class as students develop independent study skills and learner autonomy.

Implementing the route to resolution

The route to resolution policy for the management of group work projects has been implemented following the steps outlined in Table 3. Once the project groups have been assigned, groups minute their meetings on a Group Report Form summarizing the discussion, assignment of tasks and any disagreements. This Report Form is copied to the tutor, and if a disagreement arises, the students consult their tutor. Then the group tries to resolve the dispute. If this fails, the tutor is notified and meets the group to mediate and resolve the problem. This process has been able to nip many potential problems in the bud. However, if the problem continues, the group is given an Issue Form on which to outline the problem and explain what has been done to try to resolve it. This is handed to the tutor along with the Group Report Form the day before the assessment. At this point the tutor weighs the evidence and may decide to dock marks.

Table 3 Route to resolution

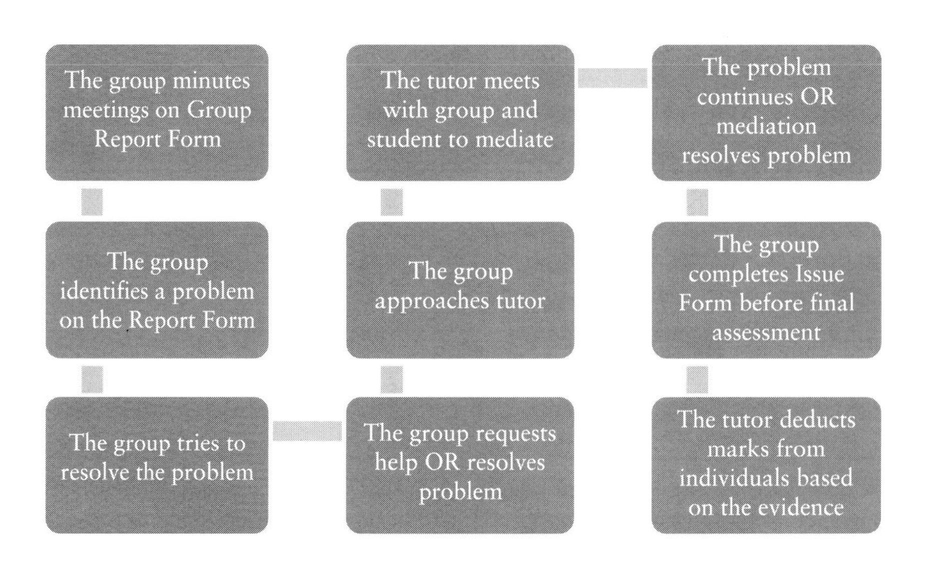

Alongside this policy, in the second stage, OCS classroom activities increase students' awareness of the rationale for group work, and promote interpersonal interaction, collaboration and teamwork through seminar discussion, and the exchange and negotiation of ideas and opinions. In two OCS group projects, students follow the route to resolution and practise group work skills, presentation skills and transferable speaking skills. In order to prepare for group work and avoid possible conflicts, in the first weeks of term, class group cohesion is developed by moving students around until they get to know their classmates (Finkbeiner, 2008). Then, through a sequence of structured classroom tasks, students identify benefits, typical group behaviours, and role-play likely problematic scenarios. In their assigned project groups, they prepare ground rules and allocate tasks and, after the Group Record Sheet is explained, they take minutes of their meetings.

In OCS semester one, mixed groups select an aspect of university study for a group survey project. They prepare questions, pilot their questionnaires, retell incidents from the interview process, and explain their data. Although Oxford (2006) concludes that there is no consensus about the best way to sequence tasks or the criteria for sequencing elements of tasks, OCS classroom support logically mirrors the survey research process. In addition, the Introduction to Information Technology module teaches students to use Excel to create graphs and visuals to illustrate their data and PowerPoint for presentations. The survey project culminates in a final assessed group presentation, which according to CDELL (2002:17), includes 'making a presentation to an audience of peers, being able to discuss technical issues, being able to explain concepts and ideas, the use of images to illustrate the spoken word, and listening to others and reacting to what they say'.

The semester two OCS group project familiarizes students with case studies which are frequently used in professional schools to provide a window into the real world by exploring a particular subject or organization to develop problem-solving, critical thinking, reflection and discussion (Jackson, 2002; Keily, 2004). In the case study project, students select a 'real world' organization, NGO or project, such as Starbucks or Toyota, to investigate. Colbeck, Campbell & Bjorklund (2000:70) found that 'students liked working on "real world projects" ... problems faced by industry that had many possible solutions, and where the focus was more on the problem-solving process than on calculating a predetermined right answer.' A case study of the Cadbury Company and a SWOT analysis illustrate the process in class, and scaffolded tasks develop group rules, role-play avoiding or resolving potential disputes, and encourage group collaboration and autonomy. Students acting as consultants write a project proposal submission, research the organization via its website and news reports, and identify recent issues affecting the organization to identify one major problem. They research its causes, recommend and evaluate three possible solutions and finally agree on 'their best solution' for the organization's problem.

Throughout both semesters, students are encouraged to reflect on their group's dynamics and their own participation. As Skehan (1998:37) points out that 'producing speech seems to be much more a case of improvizing on a clause-by-clause basis, using lexical elements (lexicalized sentence stems, or lexical phrases) wherever possible, to minimize processing demands,' functional language assists students with conversation routines. In addition, Ellis (2005:3) prioritizes instruction that ensures 'learners develop both a rich repertoire of formulaic expressions and a rule-based competency'. So, in semester one, fixed phrases help students to engage and agree, and later to challenge constructively, mediate or evaluate. Lexical phrases also provide slots which can be changed to create a variety of variable expressions. These assist less talkative students with strategies and language to take their turns and help build confidence.

Evidence of learning for both OCS projects is assessed by means of typical academic oral presentation, for which a structure is recommended, and all members must contribute for a specified time. As university assessment has traditionally been based on individual achievement, there was much debate about the division of the presentation mark between the individual and the group. The group mark promotes group interaction and collaboration, yet it may boost a weak student or penalize a more capable student. At present, two tutors assess communication (combining communication and organization), language (combining vocabulary and grammar) and group contribution (combining content and overall structure) following a set of descriptors. The group contribution mark is worth 30% and the individual mark combines communication and language for 70%. Peer assessment has been contemplated, but some foundation students lack the maturity for it. However, the project groups complete a year-end assessed discussion in which the 30% group mark reflects, to some extent, the level of cooperation and communication achieved.

The third stage of the route to resolution integrates group projects into the content modules. These group projects complement the collaboration begun in the OCS module. In the first semester, the Introduction to Information Technology module, which is taken by both business and social science students, includes a group investigation of an IT company, with students producing an executive summary and presenting their findings to both their tutor and the OCS tutor. In the second semester, Introduction to Business Methods includes a group project and presentation, while the Media and Texts: Culture module, for the social science students, includes a written group assignment. In these modules, students are grouped within their business or social science speciality programme (see Table 2) and follow the same route to resolution.

Conclusion

Although assessed group projects have many advantages, young international foundation students are often more familiar with an individually focused, teacher-led approach to learning. So the Foundation Certificate Programme combines the development of effective teamwork with a three-pronged route to resolution, which addresses the management of group projects to reduce the occurrence of group disagreements. Ehrman & Dörnyei (1998:128) indicate that resolving disagreements, triggered by factors such as uncommitted students, time management disputes or bossy leaders, encourages group stability, collaboration and the sharing of experience, perspectives and alternatives. Firstly, a managed process provides a route for solving group problems across both EAP and content modules. Secondly, the Oral Communication and Study (OCS) module develops group dynamics and cooperation in preparation for assessed group projects. Finally, the procedure is extended and integrated into the content modules, so all module tutors are more aware of the importance of group project design and monitoring, and students are not just left to work issues out by themselves.

References

Basturkmen, H. (1999). Discourse in MBA seminars: towards a description for pedagogical purposes. *English for Specific Purposes, 21*, 233–242.

Basturkmen, H. (2002). Negotiating meaning in seminar-type discussion and EAP. *English for Specific Purposes, 21/2*, 233–242.

CDELL (2002). *Introducing and supporting key skills in higher education: agenda, ideas and issues for university departments.* Centre for Developing and Evaluation Lifelong Learning, School of Education, University of Nottingham. Retrieved 11 April 2010 from http://www.nottingham.ac.uk/shared/sharedcdell/pdf-reports/keyskillspack.pdf.

Colbeck, C. L., Campbell, C. E. and Bjorklund, S. A. (2000). Grouping in the dark: What college students learn from group projects. *Journal of Higher Education, 71/1*, 60–83.

Ehrman, M. E. and Dörnyei, Z. (1998). *Interpersonal dynamics in second language education.* London: Sage Publications.

Ellis, R. (2005). *Instructed second language acquisition: A literature review.* Research Division, New Zealand Ministry of Education. Retrieved 11 April 2010 from http://www.stanford.edu/~hakuta/Courses/Ed388%20Website/Resources/Ellis%20Instructed-second-language%20-%20latest%20version.pdf.

Finkbeiner, C. (2008). Culture and good language learners. In C. Griffiths (Ed.), *Lessons from good language learners*, (pp. 35–48). Cambridge: Cambridge University Press.

Flowerdew, L. (1998). A cultural perspective on group work. *English Language Teaching Journal, 52/4*, 323–329.

Jackson, J. (2002). The China Strategy: A tale of two case leaders. *English for Specific Purposes, 21*, 243–259.

Keily, R. (2004). Learning to critique in EAP. *Journal of English for Academic Purposes 3,* 211–227.

Leki, I. (2001). A narrow thinking system: Nonnative-English-speaking students in group projects across the curriculum. *TESOL Quarterly, 35/1*, 39–67.

Oxford, R. (2006). Task based language teaching and learning: an overview. *Asian EFL Journal, 8/3, 2006 Conference Proceedings: Task-based Learning in the Asian Context.* (pp. 94–121).

Robinson, P., Strong, G., Whittle, J. & Nobe S. (2001). The development of EAP oral discussion ability. In J. Flowerdew & M. Peacock, (Eds.), *Research perspectives on English for academic purposes,* (pp. 347–360). Cambridge: Cambridge University Press.

Skehan, P. (1998) *A cognitive approach to language learning.* Oxford: Oxford University Press.

Summers, M. & Volet, S. (2008). Students' attitudes towards culturally mixed groups on international campuses: impact of participation in diverse and non-diverse groups. *Studies in Higher Education. 33/4*, 357–370.

Thondhlana, J. & Gao, X. (2009). *Needs analysis project: Phase 1 report.* Centre for English Language Education, University of Nottingham.

Zhengdong, G., Davidson, C. & Hamp-Lyons, L. (2008). Topic negotiation in peer group oral assessment situation: a conversation analytic approach. *Applied Linguistics, 30/3*, 315–334.

JOHN SLAGHT

LEAD ROLE OR SUPPORTING ACT? THE STATUS OF COMPUTER-BASED TESTING IN EAP ASSESSMENT

INTRODUCTION

Developments in high stakes online testing are relatively new: the Graduate Management Admissions Test (GMAT) version was introduced in 1999, the Graduate Record Examination (GRE) version in 2008, and The Test of English as Foreign Language (TOEFL) in the same year as the Pearson Test of English (PTE) in 2008. There are strong claims both in the literature and from organizations currently producing new online tests, such as Pearson (PTE), that the benefits of online test delivery are varied and plentiful. It has been pointed out with reasonable justification that the online test, especially the computer-adaptive online test, provides accurate reporting of results, efficient and highly reliable scoring, quick feedback and is motivating for students (Pearson, 2008). Automatic scoring of the writing test has a reliability of 0.91, which exceeds the reliability of the writing section of many other large-scale tests (De Jong, 2009). However, David Williamson[1] (2010), while acknowledging the benefits, suggests caution before full acceptance of automated online scoring. He suggests that automated scoring has inevitable limitations at this stage in terms of construct, reliability, validity and the reaction of candidates for such tests.

CERTAIN BENEFITS OF COMPUTER-BASED TESTING (CBT)

The literature suggests that online tests can effectively more than match traditional pencil-and-paper assessment in a variety of ways (Davidson, 2009; Jamieson, 2005). A relevant example is that very quick decisions can be made about whether a student should be accepted on a pre-sessional course, for

[1] David Williamson is Research Director of the English Testing System, as mentioned in online L-Test-L correspondence.

example through an online placement test. However, the level of language should be sufficiently broad to encompass the language needs of the test-taker's academic future. The use of CBT would prove a very convenient way of placing students in individual skill groups according to level once arrived on a pre-sessional. This is providing that the test is relevant to all the skills being taught on the specific course. A blended approach using both online and pencil-and-paper assessment measures might be a further consideration in this context because of the cost or the extent of testing involved. Convenience has also been suggested as a significant attribute because such tests can be administered where and when it suits the administrator and, to a degree, the test-taker.

Apart from providing relatively immediate and detailed feedback, computer-adaptive testing could provide important information for diagnostic purposes. With appropriate software and sufficient access to computer facilities, students could be tested diagnostically through CBT at every stage of formative and summative testing. Claims made, for example by Cambridge ESOL, that quick and accurate feedback and turnaround of results can enable a new curriculum to be designed or possibly re-designed at short notice are compelling. It would be undoubtedly beneficial, if sufficient course materials and resources were available, to re-organize a curriculum quickly or to design a programme specifically tailored to suit individual students' or group needs.

There is a range of potential uses to be made of online testing, including supervized examinations, continuous assessment, self-assessment and self-diagnosis. Levy's conclusions (1997), based on the results of an extensive survey amongst language teaching academics and students, identified individualization and autonomy as being particularly beneficial. Felix (2008) suggested e-journalling or e-portfolios could be exploited successfully for continuous assessment purposes. He also identified the potential for creating a new range of task types. Another benefit of CBT is that it offers students the opportunity for self-diagnosis of their language level. This form of online assessment is widely available, although the reliability of such measures can vary considerably and they are generally provided for commercial purposes.

In sum, what all this amounts to is savings in time, energy and (arguably) expense for all interested stakeholders and, as Pearson claimed during their launch in 2008, test-takers may find online testing motivating. However, it is important to consider whether the apparent accuracy, efficiency, speed and innovation provided by online testing is relevant to the needs of the key EAP stakeholders: students, academic staff, admissions staff or sponsors.

Certain problems associated with online testing

There are associated problems. One logistical problem is the number of students on a course in relation to the availability of computer stations during a test administration. A further concern is the enormity of the item bank which is apparently required for computer-adaptive testing based on item response theory (IRT). This focuses on individual items, as opposed to the test-level focus of traditional test theory, by comparing the response of each individual candidate to each item in the test. Items are generated depending on the accuracy of a candidate's response to each individual item in a test thus the need for such a large item bank. The question is whether the financial and logistical strain on course providers is justifiable, or indeed whether the inevitability of an even greater influence being wielded by powerful 'external testing systems' should be tolerated. A further logistical and contextual problem relates to the restrictions on resources and the type of location needed for large-scale online administrations. Currently, for example, CBT is often administered in centres similar to those where driving theory tests are taken. Therefore, cost might prove to be a major drawback for any but large-scale testing bodies to provide such a resource. For internal assessment this might not be a viable option on EAP courses.

At the speculative level, as students become increasingly IT literate there could be increasing expectation that tests should be delivered online just as much as the curriculum might be. Consequently, CBT could create a negative attitude to non-computer-based course design. The digitally-based upbringing of many students could result in electronic written communication being expected as a matter of course, as would be the delivery of electronic oral communication such as Skype. As automated scoring becomes more widespread, students will also learn, or may be taught, to adapt their responses to this form of scoring in order to achieve the best possible results. Problems with automated scoring related to this behavioural response may begin to emerge as examination candidates increasingly shape responses to suit the computer-based marking system.

A further concern is the possible increasing expectation and demand among students for multiple-choice style examination preparation to the neglect of 'higher order' skills such as extensive reading, listening and reading for an authentic academic purpose, or an integrated or topic-based approach. However, the more recent developments in CBT and claims made by Pearson Test of English representatives (2008) and others indicate that this is increasingly less likely to be the case.

The physical demands of taking a test online can pose problems. One pre-sessional student at the University of Reading recently responded retrospectively after taking the Pearson Test of English:

> 'I found it difficult to concentrate in front of a computer. I prefer a paper test because I can't type fast although I've been using a PC for seven or eight years. I wrote down notes by hand then tried to transfer them to the computer but I ran out of time. I found it tough in the Speaking and Writing sections. But many different question types are asked and that's good for evaluating language skills.'

This comment does not necessarily match the research conclusions put forward by Pearson, although no direct mention of the physical issues is made by the test provider.

Discussion

In the light of the issues addressed above, it is worth considering the needs of EAP students beyond technology in relation to the extent to which CBT has a role in EAP assessment. An example is the need for face-to-face interaction. At university, participating in live seminars and tutorials has always been and, it is reasonable to assume, would continue to be a crucial element of academic life. Thus there is a reason to believe that live oral assessment with a human interlocutor serves a more authentic measure. Listening and responding to live lectures remains a skill to be nurtured, and may not be sufficiently assessed by electronic means. At the same time, the use of paper sources may be considered essential, whether for the purposes of integrating and synthesizing information and ideas, or simply to develop skills such as annotating, note-taking during a lecture, or even the practical issue of comparing two or more written sources side by side.

Yet, as Crystal (2005) suggests, technology is actually changing the way language is used and therefore the abilities required to use it. Presumably, therefore, anyone not competent in using technology is not competent in communication in many situations, and the need for devising ways of assessing communicative competence in the digital age is apparent. As suggested by Chapelle & Douglas (2006), there is indeed a 'need to consider the nature of the language abilities that are called upon in technology-mediated interactions and communication, and therefore the need to rethink test constructs'. Inevitably, the evolution of technology will lead to new configurations of testing methods, and this may have an impact on test-takers' performances. Accordingly, the use of new configurations needs to be considered. Slides, for example, could be effectively and authentically used during an online listening test involving part of a lecture. However, Coniam (2001) suggests that test validity may be compromised by the inclusion of visual support in a test. There are certainly variables involved, such as the distraction of viewing and typing responses simultaneously, unless time is factored into the test to allow transcription from handwritten notes to the screen. Such compromises may be the way forward as the level of keyboarding skills could impact on candidate performance.

Further test configurations that could be comfortably adapted or developed particularly for EAP purposes include gap-fill completion tasks such as the C-Test format, bibliography re-ordering tasks or re-ordering at sentence or paragraph level. Also access could be made available to electronic sources for selective or comparative reading, as could drag-and-drop configurations for summary-completion or syntax-related activities.

However, there are further implications involved with the introduction of new electronically-directed configurations. Dillon (1992) and Sawaki (2001) contest that reading on screen is 25% slower than paper. Given that students on HE courses may be expected to read literally hundreds of pages per week, this is a significant issue. Short online reading texts, provided simply for convenience, could lead to a de-sensitizing of students to the demands of a heavy reading load on academic courses. The need to scroll backwards and forwards with longer scripts online would be expected to slow up the process of reading rather than facilitate it, and would seem to put further strain on the candidate no matter how authentic the activity. The argument against using drag-and-drop is that it may encourage the tendency to plagiarize. It would certainly seem to discourage candidates from generating language in order to express ideas in their own words.

Online testing of oral ability suggests a number of potential areas for debate. There is an argument that interacting with a machine is a counterintuitive process because the interaction is essentially mono-directional: the computer initiates, the candidate responds. Therein lies a lack of precision (Chapelle & Douglas, 2006). The computer, currently at least, cannot probe, re-phrase or account for culturally bound pauses. There are cultures where it is customary to pause before giving a considered response; not to do so is considered at least impolite. The reaction of the Reading University student mentioned earlier does suggest that pausing for consideration might be a stumbling block in assessing the online approximation of two-way interaction, as each response has to be initiated within a few seconds. A positive benefit, however, is the expanded possibilities for identifying and/or diagnosing specific spoken language problems. For example, the sophistication of modern technology allows for greater accuracy in analyzing the production of discrete sounds, especially for diagnostic or formative purposes.

Need is a fundamental factor in assessing the potential status of online testing for academic purposes. Distance learning courses are almost entirely delivered electronically. In this case, it would seem logical that assessment should be similarly carried out. With a traditional pre-sessional course delivered in situ, however, online testing may be less relevant to the needs of the participants. It depends very much on the rationale behind and the content of a pre-sessional course. The aim of the majority of such courses is to prepare international students to work on a level playing field within the academic community that they are destined to join. It should not be considered a test preparation course, although an exit test may be an element in assessing a student's ability to benefit fully from a future academic course.

How much online assessment is an appropriate assessment measure on many language and study skills EAP courses needs to be carefully weighed. Decisions also need to be made about the impact of technology on academic language testing. It is a revolutionary development in some senses. Key stakeholders should be confident that it is a medium of test delivery which is not only logistically sound in terms of delivery, rating and turnaround, but that it is fair and necessary given the needs, experience and motivation of the students, the most relevant stakeholders of all. At the same time, the impact of technology on language in general is also a factor and in this case, intuitively, there would seem to be a certain logic in using technology to assess language.

The power wielded by commercially influenced, electronically delivered course content and assessment adds fuel to the test-driven course versus the course-driven test debate. The expense and logistical demands of creating a suitable online in-house version of a pre-sessional exit test would be a major constraint in many situations. As a result, a neatly packaged, efficient and pedagogically sound external online assessment measure may seem a compelling alternative. However, a test must suit the needs of the test-taker and not drive those needs.

Fairness and accuracy of assessment are essential in any high stakes testing situation. The accuracy of automated marking and the results of 'person-independent' rating published by Pearson (2008) claims that:

> ... the correlation of ... overall scores [by summing the trait scores for each candidate across all of the written items] ...

> between pairs of raters was 0.87. The correlation between the human score and the machine-generated score was 0.88. The reliability of the measure of writing in PTE is 0.89.

This is impressive and should certainly ensure enhanced fairness in rating. It does beg the question, however, of whether it reflects the kind of idiosyncratic marking that international students may experience once embarked on further academic studies. University lecturers are likely to have a number of different approaches to marking extended texts such as projects or dissertations. Individual and inter-rater reliability is generally not going to be nearly as accurate as technology-driven scoring. Reliance on the electronic form of assessment may prove problematic as a result. The marking of essays during an EAP pre-sessional course needs to be standardized to ensure fair and accurate marking between teachers and arguably mitigates against e-marking during a course.

A final thought is reserved for the test-taker. What does the student prefer and how demanding is an online test? The Pearson Test of English, for example, takes three hours to complete because of its skills-integrated approach and its wide-ranging assessment of skills through a battery of task types. Physically, this is a demanding challenge despite the opportunity to take a ten-minute break at a certain stage of the test. There are further implications involved in the introduction of new electronically-directed configurations. Reference has already been made to the views of Dillan (1992) and Sawaki (2001) regarding the impact of on-screen reading. It would certainly suggest that adjustments to the format and timing of tests of academic reading would need to be implemented.

Also with regard to test-takers, it is fair to assume that online tests may be motivating simply because they embrace technology. These measures could also help eliminate the physical effort involved in completing traditional pencil-and-paper tests, which may be particularly significant with the generation of digital natives now taking language tests. It may be that, by simply providing sufficient breaks between sections of a test, the physical and mental demands posed by focusing on a screen for up to three hours can be alleviated.

Conclusion

The benefits of CBT are significant; there are also drawbacks. These are inevitable in any system which is relatively new and is undergoing rapid development in tandem with the speed of technological developments in general. In some ways it would seem that CBT adds greater flexibility in terms of when and where tests can be administered, although test security may be a greater concern than with traditional tests because of the greater potential for unauthorized access. Nonetheless, although in terms of EAP assessment measures certain reservations have been expressed relating to the future experience of pre-sessional students once embarked on academic courses, online testing is worthy at least of a supporting role. However, its function and format require careful monitoring. The repertoire and scope of task types may also need expansion in some cases. Developments in online assessment have introduced new test formats, particularly in speaking and listening, but are limited, for example, in making use of extended texts to test EAP reading needs. Ultimately, the status and value of language assessment need to be carefully considered in relation to tried and mostly trusted traditional language testing modes. Possibly a compromise between online and traditional assessment media should be promoted through a blended approach to assessment, especially within the EAP context.

There is little doubt that online testing must be part of the future of many forms of testing, including the assessment of language, and that it is simply a question of to what extent. Alderson (2005) refers to Bennett (1998), who saw computer-based assessment developing over three phases. Firstly, the replication of paper-and-pencil tests. Following is the assessment of abilities and knowledge which were not previously possible. Finally, it is suggested that the assessment procedure would become embedded in the contents of language learning programmes in such a way that the language learner would not even be aware that assessment is taking place. At present, it seems that CBT of language has, at least partially, reached the second of Bennett's phases, and with careful monitoring can play a role in EAP assessment.

REFERENCES

Alderson, C. J. (2005). *Diagnosing foreign language proficiency*. UK: Continuum.

Bennett, R. E. (1998). *Reinventing assessment: speculations on the future of large-scale educational testing*. NJ: Educational Testing Service.

Cambridge ESOL (2010). http://www.cambridgeesol.org/what-we-do/exam-revisions/cbt.html.

Chapelle, C. & Douglas, D. (2006). *Assessing language through computer technology*. Cambridge: Cambridge University Press.

Coniam, D. (2001). The use of audio or video comprehension as an assessment instrument in the certification of English Language Teachers: A case study. *SYSTEM, 29*, 1–14.

Crystal, D. (February 2005). The scope of internet linguistics. Paper given to the American Association for the advancement of science meeting.

Davidson, P. (February 2009). *Computerised testing: the good, the bad and the ugly*: Dubai: TESOL Arabia.

Dillon, A. (1992). Reading from paper versus screens: a critical review of the empirical literature. *Ergonomics, 35/10*, 1297–1326.

Felix, U. (2008). *The unreasonable effectiveness of CALL; what have we learned in two decades of research*. UK: EACALL, (pp. 141–161).

Jamieson, J. (2005). Trends in computer-based second language assessment. *Annual Review of Applied Linguistics, 25*, 228–242. Cambridge: Cambridge University Press.

Levy, M. (1997). *Computer-assisted language learning: concept & conceptualisation*. Oxford: Clarendon Press.

Pearson Test of English (PTE) and automated scoring (November 2008). UK: Pearson Language Tests.

Sawaki, Y. (2001). Comparability of Conventional and Computerized Tests of Reading in a Second Language. *Language Learning & Technology, 5*.

Jane Nolan and Elizabeth Poynter

Teacher! How can I improve my writing?

Introduction

In HE pre-sessional EAP courses, students need to respond effectively to tutor feedback on their writing within the limited time period of such courses. Despite the frequency that we as teachers are asked by students how they can improve their writing, our experience at Leeds Met is that students do not always take in, or respond effectively to, detailed teacher feedback. Indeed, research suggests that even rich, high-quality feedback may be 'lost in translation' and not easily understood by students (Carless, 2006:233), who, in general, report a less than satisfactory experience of receiving feedback on their work (Race, 2007:86). There is obviously more to the process than the teacher simply 'transmitting' feedback to students about the strengths and weaknesses in their writing and expecting them to make immediate use of it to improve their work.

This paper will examine more closely the issues we found, and discuss the outcomes of a project to improve tutor feedback and student response to the feedback on their academic writing in the university's pre-sessional EAP courses.

Formative assessment and assessment for learning

While assessment may dictate 'what students regard as important' (Brown & Knight, 1994:2) the key focus of this study is the role of formative assessment, defined as 'all those activities undertaken by teachers and/or by their students, which provide information to be used as feedback to modify the teaching and learning activities in which they are engaged' (Black & Wiliam, 1998:9–10). It is also now common to hear the term 'assessment for learning' being used with a very similar meaning (Asghar et al., 2008). The concept of assessment for learning explicitly includes the idea of fostering student development, through supporting students to take responsibility for 'evaluating, judging and improving their own performance, by actively using a range of feedback' (McDowell et al., 2006:3). Gauging the provision of this support and gradually withdrawing it until students are able to 'direct their own learning' (ibid.) is therefore a key feature of course design.

Self-directed learning is one of the six key conditions for the effective use of 'assessment for learning' as outlined by the Northumbria Centre for Excellence in Teaching and Learning (see Figure 1). In the context of university pre-sessional EAP courses, some of these conditions naturally fit together in terms of the learning and assessment that students undertake.

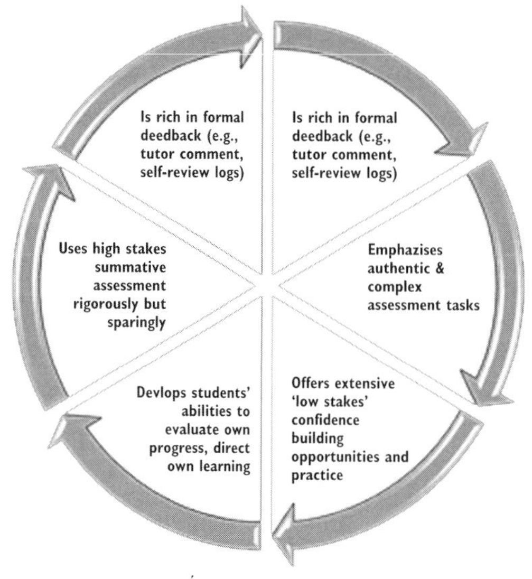

Figure 1 The six key conditions for the support of Assessment for Learning in a learning environment (McDowell et al., 2006:4)

Extensive low-stakes opportunities for students to develop and practise their skills

'This can usefully be done with students working cooperatively together, supporting and giving feedback to each other, receiving a wide range of formal and informal feedback on their progress, in order to build confidence and achievement' (ibid.). This might take the form of short pieces of academic writing in English or practice of a range of different genres of writing, which are not summatively assessed or graded.

Opportunities to engage in authentic and complex tasks

There is a significant amount of evidence that students engage more actively with challenging activities. In conjunction with regular formal feedback on their work, e.g., tutor comments on the work at a formative stage, complex tasks and feedback together have been found to be 'directly related with high achievement' (Black & Wiliam, 1998:38). In pre-sessional courses, such authentic tasks may include the carrying out of a longer piece of academic work or project-type work, which can be summatively assessed at the end of the course, a way of using 'high-stakes summative assessment rigorously but sparingly rather than as the main driver for learning' (McDowell et al., 2006:4).

Student benefit from feedback

Sadler (1989) suggests that, in order for students to benefit from feedback on academic tasks, they need to have a clear understanding of the target or goal being aimed for, how their current performance relates to achieving that, and how they can close the gap between the two. However, Nicol & Macfarlane-Dick (2006:201) suggest that 'feedback messages are invariably complex and difficult to decipher' and that, in order to make use of the feedback, students need to be able to interpret and make active sense of it (Black & Wiliam, 1998:10). Another key element in responding to feedback is related to the motivations and self-perceptions of students, e.g., their beliefs about learning and their capacity to respond. Research on the affective aspect of feedback shows that it can influence how positive or negative students feel, as well as 'what and how they learn' (Nicol & Macfarlane-Dick 2006:201). Therefore, the links between the way the message or feedback is received, the motivation to choose between different responses to it, and the learning activity which results (or not) are complex (Black & Wiliam, 1998), and 'interpersonal considerations' in the relationship between the teacher and learner may have been underestimated (Hyland & Hyland, 2006:222).

Giving effective feedback

Research cited by Nicol & Macfarlane-Dick, (2006:199–204) has shown that 'students can learn to be more self-regulated', for example to 'generate internal feedback as they monitor their engagement with learning activities and tasks, and assess progress towards goals'. High-quality feedback, which is part of an ongoing dialogue between teachers and students, supports students' motivation and positive attitudes to learning, and helps them develop skills for self-assessment and reflection on their learning; in making clear what good performance on a task is, providing opportunities to close the gap in terms of current performance and future goals through detailed information to students about their learning, it can assist learners in becoming more self-regulated (ibid.:205). Students also need to be given an opportunity to improve the work, e.g., repeating the same task, or taking the knowledge gained forward to the next (Boud, 2000).

Methodology

Using the categories of McDowell et al. (2006) for effective assessment for learning, this report looks firstly at weekly written feedback on writing tasks which are designed to offer extensive low-stakes opportunities for practice and to develop students' abilities to direct their own learning, and then at giving audio feedback on a longer project in which students work towards a 2,000–4,000 word project involving primary or secondary research or both, depending on the length of the course. This offers an 'authentic and complex' task (ibid.), as well as opportunities to submit multiple drafts in response to feedback, before the project is summatively assessed. Students' opinions on both the written and audio feedback were gathered over an 18-month period.

Initially, online questionnaires in relation to weekly written feedback were administered using Snap9 (Snap survey software, 2009 – see appendix). Two cohorts of former pre-sessional students who had left the department to go on to their Master's courses were e-mailed with a link to the questionnaire, which could then be returned anonymously. This method was used firstly because it was quick and simple for the students to complete, encouraging response, and secondly because e-mail contact was the most efficient way of contacting former students. The online questionnaires consisted of multiple-choice questions and collected quantitative data only (see Appendix 1). Students' attitudes to the feedback they had received on individual assignments, the error-recognition work in class, whether students had used the feedback when writing the next assignment (and subsequently on their Master's course), and whether they felt it had helped them to write better, were surveyed. Similar questionnaires distributed by Snap9 were also used to gather responses from the summer pre-sessional students after subsequent changes to feedback on weekly writing assignments, and again after the students had gone on to their Master's courses.

Student responses to audio feedback have so far been collected in situ, using a questionnaire containing a mixture of open and closed questions to collect both qualitative and quantitative data.

This is an ongoing, action research style project (Robson, 2002:217), with responses to the questionnaires being used to adjust and focus tutor feedback in terms of content and the techniques used, in order to support students in responding to the feedback and motivate them to take control of improving their academic writing. This is detailed below.

Weekly written feedback

Feedback on the weekly writing assignments had consisted of the following: errors highlighted on the individual script, with a correction code in the margin; comments on each script on the broad areas of accuracy, range, content and structure; and error recognition group work in the following class. Over time, the proportion of accuracy work was decreased and it was hoped that the combination of individual help on the script with group work on error recognition would enable the students to develop awareness of their own strengths and weaknesses. Teachers' subjective impressions, however, suggested that students were not using feedback as effectively as they might. The same types of error were frequently commented on week after week, including points which had been discussed in the previous class. Therefore, two case studies were carried out to test this impression, some changes were made to the feedback method and student attitudes to feedback were surveyed.

Case studies

The weekly written work of two students on our one-semester pre-sessional course was analyzed.

Student A, from India, revealed the following typical errors:

- nouns unmarked for plural number
- missing third-person singular -s
- use of past tense instead of present simple
- difficulties with multi-verb structures, e.g., 'should be take care to separated'
- proofreading
- paragraphing (some paragraphs had two topic sentences and no development)

Focusing on these specific points over three assignments produced some improvement. The number of unmarked plurals went from 7 out of 16, to 6 out of 29, to 1 out of 42, for instance. There was a similar reduction in missing third-person -s and inappropriate past tenses, but in the second assignment a new problem occurred, namely 'be' + verb, e.g., 'it's save time', 'are depends on', which was even more numerous in the third. The proofreading did improve, but the paragraphing continued to be weak.

Student B, from China, produced work at a higher level initially, with good accuracy and command of, for instance, passives. The chief problems were with spelling, wrong parts of speech and definite articles. While the spelling and articles improved, she continued to use adjectives for nouns or verbs, etc., but not the same specific words: for example, she wrote 'to broad your horizon' in assignment one, but 'broaden your horizons' in assignment two. Clearly within such a short time frame (one month) it is not easy to identify improvement in specific vocabulary/structures, but this suggests that the feedback is succeeding to some extent.

Changes to feedback method

A new style of feedback was introduced on the pre-sessional course in the summer of 2008, in an attempt to help students focus better on their strengths and weaknesses. For the first assignment, they were asked to grade themselves on content, structure, accuracy and range; these grades could then be compared with that of the teacher, in order to select some points to work on in the next assignment. For subsequent assignments, students identified up to four things they were going to work on, before writing, and commented afterwards on how well they felt they had succeeded. These might include specific accuracy points, paragraphing, conclusions, academic register and so on. The tutor was then able to focus on these specific aspects of the assignment when giving feedback.

Student surveys

Six students out of a possible 13 (two cohorts) responded to the first questionnaire, mostly agreeing that the individual feedback was 'helpful and sufficient'. Most continued to use it on their Master's programme (three 'usually' and three 'once or twice') and felt it helped them to write better assignments (three 'definitely' and three 'maybe').

Only 3 summer pre-sessional students out of 11 responded: they were mostly positive, but indicated that they had found the new feedback method quite difficult. This tallied with teachers' impressions of the new system. The feedback sheets had been intended to help the students to take more responsibility for their own learning, but they seemed to find it difficult to know what points to work on. Two Thai students, for example, repeatedly identified tenses as a weakness to work on, despite the fact that they were not having many errors in this area highlighted; the conclusion was that they were probably basing their decisions on their previous language-learning experience rather than on an analysis of their current work.

The results of the two surveys, however limited in validity by small numbers, suggested that students were quite satisfied with correction code and error recognition work as tools to improve their written English. At the same time, they seemed to find it difficult to judge for themselves where their strengths and weaknesses lay, and expecting them to make such a judgement from the outset was maybe too demanding. The next step, therefore, was to adjust the feedback in an attempt to develop this judgement skill more incrementally.

The next step

In semester two of the academic year 2008–2009, while the marking-up of scripts continued as before, for each student a maximum of three recommendations was made after each assignment, for the first four assignments. These might all be accuracy points for students whose chief weakness lay in this area, but might also include such suggestions as focusing on a good introduction, on developing content points, or on avoiding irrelevancy. In class, after these four assignments, a list of possible weaknesses was looked at and action points suggested for each. Students were also given a grid with a list of possible accuracy errors, and required to count the total number of each type in each of the first four assignments and fill in the numbers on the grid, thus enabling them to identify their main problem areas. This technique has been used successfully by our Spanish tutors to improve the writing skills of British students in Spanish.

From the fifth assignment onwards, students were then asked to fill in their own three points to focus on, choosing from the list they had been given. This might be three accuracy points, if they had found a large number of errors on their grid. They were further asked to write their chosen three things at the top of their assignment so that feedback could be specifically directed to those areas. Those students who actually did all three successfully identified suitable points of weakness on which to focus – far more successfully than the summer students, with less help, had done. One in particular also used this to improve his writing quite considerably (see Figure 2 below).

Accuracy	Quite good. You are still doing quite well with the countable/ uncountable nouns (but check 'technology'), and prepositions are fine. One or two errors with articles still, but it is not a major problem.
Content	You have developed your points fairly well. However, you have NOT answered the question, which told you to agree with the statement. Do be careful about this.
Structure	A nice clear structure for an argument essay, with appropriate paragraphing.
Range of language	I think this is improving. The fact that there are several problems with vocab. just means you are experimenting – don't worry, just try to learn from your mistakes.
Recommendations for next time	1 2 3

Figure 2 Sample feedback sheet from a student [Student had chosen to focus on: 1. Developing points; 2. Using a wide range of vocabulary; 3. Prepositions and articles (N.B. this should really have been two points)]

Appropriately identifying 'Developing points', 'Using a wide range of vocabulary', and 'Prepositions and articles' as areas of focus, this student managed to address all these, reducing the number of accuracy errors and improving the content and range of language. Notably, he maintained progress in an area from week to week, while also successfully moving on to address a new point.

Using audio feedback

While written feedback was used to give regular feedback on language accuracy, audio feedback was used to give feedback on students' extended research projects and more general academic skills, e.g., critical thinking or academic referencing.

The 'Sounds Good' project, exploring the effectiveness of using digital audio to give assessment feedback, ran at Leeds Metropolitan University from January 2008 until February 2009, aiming to investigate whether audio feedback provided richer feedback to students 'as speech is potentially a richer medium than written text' (Rotherham, 2009). Responses from 1,201 students in different faculties were extremely positive, as students considered the audio feedback more personal and detailed than written feedback, as well as being evidence that the lecturer had carefully considered their work (ibid.). Another advantage of audio for staff was the possibility of giving a substantial amount of feedback to a student in a shorter time than it might take to write it. This was an attraction when considering giving extensive and complex feedback on students' research project proposals and drafts.

Formative feedback was given on the final drafts of project proposals, summing up comments after one-to-one feedback sessions which allowed students to ask questions. Summative feedback was given on the proposal itself once submitted, this time in both written and oral form. The audio feedback fed forward to the writing up of the final project. The MP3 files could be either sent to the students by e-mail or uploaded through the VLE. Audio feedback was similarly given to two cohorts of pre-sessional students on final drafts of the projects as they were written up.

The first cohort was surveyed on their responses to audio feedback on their research proposals and final projects. Six out of eight students were present at the end of the course to complete the questionnaire, and responses were then numbered and coded.

All students found the MP3 files easy to access and use, and all listened to the files more than once, the majority making notes from the comments and claiming to use them to improve their drafts. In responses to the open questions several students suggested that audio-feedback 'contains more information than written feedback' (S3), and 'it's easier to understand' (S4), as 'students can listen to it again and again' (S1), making it also a 'good way to practise listening' (S6). Particularly interesting responses included 'it gives me right direction for my project' (S5), 'it's a brilliant way to push me' (S2), and 'no excuse not to do the work' (S2). It does seem, that for a number of students, audio feedback, which is spoken and so would generally be expressed in simpler language than written feedback, allows them to actively make sense of the feedback and seems possibly also to motivate them to act on it (Black &

Wiliam, 1998). Other research, e.g., Sipple (2007), has also highlighted how personal and affective factors are stronger in audio feedback, increasing students' perceptions of their motivation, their self-confidence and a more personal student-teacher relationship.

Conclusion

Clearly this is still a work in progress, and the small numbers of the cohorts make any conclusions tentative at best, but the results on the latest feedback approach, which offers considerable support to students in identifying their strengths and weaknesses, are encouraging so far. Similarly, audio feedback seems to better enable students to make sense of and interpret feedback. Overall, a range of feedback mechanisms may be important to help all students to improve, but in particular, feedback mechanisms that actively engage students may be most successful in supporting them in judging and improving their achievement in writing. Work on this study will continue, with a questionnaire on both audio and written feedback, similar to those described above, administered to the latest pre-sessional cohort once they have commenced their Master's programme.

References

Asghar, M., Laight, J., Aslett-Bentley, A. with Charlton, M., Clegg, S., Connell, J., Cooper, B., Dean, L., Mayfield, W., Nolan, J. and Soosay, M. (2008). Discursive communities and local practices – formative assessment as a local practice. *Conference Full Papers: Proceedings from the SRHE (Society for Research into Higher Education) Annual Conference, Valuing Higher Education*, 9–11 December, 2008, Liverpool.

Black, P. & Wiliam, D. (1998). Assessment and classroom learning. *Assessment in Education, 5/1*, 7–74.

Boud, D. (2000). Sustainable assessment: rethinking assessment for the learning society. *Studies in Continuing Education, 22/2*, 151–167.

Brown, S. & Knight, P. (1994). *Assessing Learners in Higher Education*. London: Kogan Page.

Carless, D. (2006). Differing perceptions in the feedback process. *Studies in Higher Education, 31/2*, 219–233.

Hyland, K. & Hyland, F. (2006). Interpersonal aspects of response: constructing and interpreting teacher written feedback. In K. Hyland & F. Hyland, *Feedback in Second Language Writing: Contexts and issues*. New York: Cambridge University Press.

McDowell, L. et al. (2006). *Assessment for Learning: Current Practice Exemplars from the Centre for Excellence in Teaching and Learning in Assessment for Learning*. Retrieved 2 April 2009 from: http://northumbria.ac.uk/static/5007/cetlpdf/exemplars.pdf

Nicol, D. & Macfarlane-Dick, D. (2006). Formative assessment and self-regulated learning: a model and seven principles of good feedback practice. *Studies in Higher Education, 31/2*, 199–218.

Race, P. (2007). *How to Get a Good Degree: Making the most of your time at university* (2nd edition). Open University Press/McGraw-Hill Education.

Robson, C. (2002). *Real World Research* (2nd edition). Oxford: Blackwell Publishers.

Rotherham, B. (2009). *Sounds Good Final Report*. Retrieved 2 April 2009 from http://www.jisc.ac.uk/publications/documents/soundsgoodfinalreport.aspx#downloads.

Sadler, D. R. (1989). Formative assessment and the design of instructional systems. *Instructional Science, 18*, 119–144.
Sipple, S. (2007). Ideas in practice: Developmental writers' attitudes towards audio and written feedback. *Journal of Developmental Education, 30/3*, 22–31.
Snap survey software (2009). *Campus edition.* Retrieved 2 October 2009 from
http://www.snapsurveys.com/software/softwarecampus.shtml.

Appendix I

Academic writing feedback survey

In order to improve the effectiveness of my feedback on students' writing, I would like your views. Please take a few minutes to choose the best (ONE) answer for each question below. (This survey was distributed using Snap9 software; this is a Word facsimile.)

1. Did you find the feedback written on your essays
a) too much detail ☐
b) helpful and sufficient ☐
c) not enough ☐
d) difficult to understand? ☐

2. Did you find the error recognition work we did in class
a) too much detail ☐
b) helpful and sufficient ☐
c) not enough ☐
d) difficult to understand? ☐

3. Did you try to use the feedback when writing the next assignment?
a) Always, very carefully ☐
b) Sometimes, when I remembered ☐
c) Not at all ☐

4. Did you feel that your writing had improved during the course?
a) Yes, very much ☐
b) Yes, a little ☐
c) No, not really ☐

5. After you started your Master's course, did you continue to use the feedback from the writing class to help with assignments?
a) Yes, usually ☐
b) Yes, once or twice ☐
answer question 6
c) No ☐
answer question 7

6. Did it help you to write better assignments?
a) Yes, definitely ☐
b) Maybe ☐
c) I don't think so ☐

OR

7. Why not?

a) I didn't think it would help ☐
b) It would have taken too much time ☐
c) I had lost my pre-Master's papers ☐
d) I didn't think of doing it ☐

Appendix 2

Using audio feedback

This semester I have been experimenting with using MP3 files to give students oral feedback on their work. I'd be very grateful if you could give some feedback on your responses to this.

First file, 9 March

Formative feedback on final draft of the PreMA project outline – summing up comments after 1:1 feedback session, last class before submission of outline on 13th March, sent to e-mail address.

1. Did you listen to the audio feedback? Please tick all that apply.
   - ☐ On a university computer
   - ☐ On a computer at home
   - ☐ On a computer somewhere else
   - ☐ On a portable audio player (e.g., MP3 player)
   - ☐ Some other way (please explain)
   - ☐ No

2. How easy was it to listen to the audio feedback? Please tick.
   - ☐ Very easy
   - ☐ Fairly easy
   - ☐ Neither easy nor difficult
   - ☐ Fairly difficult (please explain)
   - ☐ Very difficult/impossible (please explain)
   - ☐ Didn't/couldn't listen

3. Did you make use of the audio feedback between receiving it on the 9th and submitting your outline on 13th March? Tick all that apply.
   - ☐ Yes, I listened more than once
   - ☐ Yes, I made notes from the comments
   - ☐ Yes, I used the comments to improve my draft outline
   - ☐ Some other way (please explain)
   - ☐ No

Second file, 2nd April

Summative feedback on PreMA project outline, feeding forward to writing up of final project, both oral and written feedback, sent through e-mail.

4. Did you listen to the audio feedback? Please tick ALL that apply.
   - ☐ On a university computer
   - ☐ On a computer at home
   - ☐ On a computer somewhere else
   - ☐ On a portable audio player (e.g. MP3 player)
   - ☐ Some other way (please explain)
   - ☐ No, not yet

5. How easy was it to listen to the audio feedback? Please tick.
   - ☐ Very easy
   - ☐ Fairly easy
   - ☐ Neither easy nor difficult
   - ☐ Fairly difficult (please explain)
   - ☐ Very difficult/ impossible (please explain)
   - ☐ Didn't/couldn't listen

6. Which did you find **most** useful?
   - ☐ The audio feedback (please explain why)
   - ☐ The written feedback (please explain why)
   - ☐ Both in different ways (please explain why)

   Why?

7. How does audio feedback compare with written feedback?

8. What is your opinion on receiving audio feedback during this module?

9. Do you have any other comments about receiving audio feedback?

MANY THANKS FOR COMPLETING THIS QUESTIONNAIRE

Notes on Contributors

DOROTHY ADAMS-METAXOPOULOU is an EAP/EFL lecturer, Cambridge ESOL examiner, and writer. Her recent publications include *Link Up* for Thomson-Heinle and a grammar book for Macmillan. She has recently been appointed Head of English at Manchester Victoria College, where she delivers courses in EAP, EFL and Teacher Training.

MARY DAVIS is Senior Lecturer of EAP at Oxford Brookes University, where she leads the pre-Master's programme. She is undertaking PhD research in plagiarism education at the Institute of Education, University of London. Her research interests also include the use of Turnitin at the formative stage of academic writing.

CHRISTINE FEAK has been a lecturer at the English Language Institute, University of Michigan, since 1988, where she is the lead lecturer for academic writing courses. Her current research interests include the discourse analysis of academic writing and medical writing for research and publication.

ANDY GILLETT has spent the last 30 years teaching English and related subjects in the UK and abroad. Most recently, he has taught EAP in British higher education. His work now involves a range of projects connected with course planning, materials design & evaluation, and teaching for several clients.

JOHN HALL is Head of International Foundation Year Programmes for the Arts and Social Sciences at the University of Nottingham's Centre for English Language Education (CELE). He convenes the 'Written Communication and Study' module and is involved in foundation level curriculum development across campuses in the UK, China and Malaysia.

ANGELA HAMMOND has 30 years' experience of education in both a UK and international context. She has taught and developed research and study skills material on a range of programmes for overseas students in higher education. She currently works in the Learning and Teaching Institute at the University of Hertfordshire.

SARAH HORROD taught in Turkey and China before gaining an MA in ELT at Essex. She has worked in EAP since 1995, firstly at The School of Oriental and African Studies (SOAS) and for the last six years at Kingston. She has experience of creating and teaching a wide variety of courses including ESAP credit-bearing modules. Her interests include materials design, learner motivation and ESAP.

BRUCE HOWELL works in the International Study and Language Centre (ISLC) at the University of Reading as a teacher on EAP courses. As Assistant Director of Assessment, he leads the writing, marking and administrating of EAP tests, including the Test of English for Educational Purposes (TEEP).

KEN HYLAND is Professor of Applied Linguistics and Director of the Centre for Applied English Studies at the University of Hong Kong. He has published over 150 articles and 14 books on language education and academic writing. He was founding co-editor of the *Journal of English for Academic Purposes* and is now co-editor of *Applied Linguistics*.

YONGYAN LI is an Assistant Professor at the Faculty of Education of the University of Hong Kong. She was a Postdoctoral Fellow at the Department of English, The Hong Kong Polytechnic University from 2008 to 2009. Her research interests focus on scholarly literacy and academic writing.

JOHN MORLEY is Director of the University-wide Language Programmes at the University of Manchester. Part of this work involves organizing and running classes and workshops in academic writing for students and for staff. He holds a PhD in Applied Linguistics, and has previously taught in Australia, Singapore, Spain and Indonesia.

PHIL MORRIS has lectured in Spanish, Translation Studies and EAP at the Universities of Liverpool, Lancaster and Salamanca, and is currently Lecturer in EAP/EFL at the Manchester Metropolitan University, where he now coordinates the Language Learning Advisory Service.

PHILIP NATHAN teaches ESP, Assessment and Research Methods modules on Durham University's MA TESOL/Applied Language Studies progamme. He is also Director of the University's in-sessional support programme and pre-MBA preparatory programme. His research interests centre around the teaching and learning of academic writing, in particular academic business writing.

HILARY NESI is Professor in English Language in the Department of English and Languages at Coventry University, UK. She was Principal Investigator for the project to create the *BASE* corpus of British Academic Spoken English, and for the *BAWE* corpus project 'An Investigation of Genres of Assessed Writing in British Higher Education'.

JANE NOLAN runs Leeds Metropolitan University's pre-sessional and in-sessional academic English and study skills courses and teaches on the MA ELT. Her special interests are teaching EAP and teacher education and she has worked in teacher development in Hungary and the Czech Republic as well as the UK.

ELIZABETH POYNTER has worked at Leeds Metropolitan University for 11 years; she runs the pre-Master's programme and teaches on the pre-sessional and in-sessional courses. Her first degree was in Chinese Studies and she has worked in China, Japan and Germany. She added an MPhil in Linguistics with a special interest in phonology.

DAVID D. QIAN is Professor of Applied Linguistics at the Department of English, The Hong Kong Polytechnic University. His main research interests include language testing and assessment, second language vocabulary acquisition and measurement, and corpus linguistics.

MÜJDE ŞENER NORDLING has an MA in Language Program Management from Macquarie University. She worked as an ELT instructor in Bilkent University and Sabanci University. Her main interests are academic reading and writing, curriculum design and content-based instruction. At present, she lives in Stockholm studying Swedish.

JOHN SLAGHT is Director of Assessment and Test Development at the International Study and Language Centre, the University of Reading. He has more than 30 years' experience in language testing gained in various parts of the world.

ANN SMITH is an EAP tutor and materials developer at the University of Nottingham's Centre for English Language Education (CELE). She has extensive experience as a TESOL/EAP teacher, teacher trainer, examiner and materials developer. Her interests focus on syllabus design, group tasks, case-based teaching and classroom practice.

BENET VINCENT taught EFL and EAP in Russia, the UK and Turkey for 14 years, before recently starting a PhD in English at the University of Birmingham. His interests include Corpus Linguistics, Discourse Analysis, Writing and Vocabulary.

Acknowledgements:

I would like to thank the following people for their valuable contributions to the present volume:

The organizers of the Reading 2009 BALEAP conference; Dr Melinda Whong, my predecessor as BALEAP Publications Officer, who began the process of collecting papers together and has offered very useful advice throughout the editing process; and last, but not least, Jean McCutcheon, whose tremendous organisational skills and eye for detail have kept the publication on track. Thank you, Jean.